W9-BZL-827

WOODLAND ECOLOGY

WOODLAND
Environmental Forestry

LEON S. MINCKLER
Drawings by FRANCIS W. DAVIS

SYRACUSE UNIVERSITY PRESS 1975

ECOLOGY
for the Small Owner

Copyright © 1975 by Syracuse University Press
Syracuse, New York 13210

All Rights Reserved

First Edition
First Printing 1975
Second Printing 1975

All drawings were made by Francis W. Davis. Unless
otherwise noted, all photographs were taken by Francis
W. Davis or by Leon S. Minckler while the author was
employed by the United States Forest Service.

Library of Congress Cataloging in Publication Data

Minckler, Leon Sherwood, 1906-
    Woodland ecology.

    Bibliography: p.
    1. Wood-lots — United States. 2. Forest ecology —
United States. 3. Forest management — United States.
4. Forests and forestry — United States — Multiple use.
I. Title.
SD387.W6.M56   333.7'5'0974   74-21909
ISBN 0-8156-0109-3

Manufactured in the United States of America

This book is dedicated to my father

WALTER HARMON MINCKLER

Who taught me the old virtues

and to

MY CHILDREN AND STUDENTS

Who taught me their new meanings

Leon S. Minckler, Ph.D., worked for many years with the U.S. Forest Service at forest experiment stations, conducting research in silviculture, forest management, and the ecology of hardwood forests. He has taught at the University of Michigan, Southern Illinois University, Virginia Polytechnic Institute and State University, and State University of New York College of Environmental Science and Forestry, Syracuse, where he is Adjunct Professor.

Preface

This book will describe the important contribution of woodlands to the environmental health of an area and the personal satisfactions and economic benefits the owner can derive from a well-managed forest environment. Emphasis will be placed on providing woodland owners with an understanding of the ecological principles and human interests related to the total forest environment.

The book will endeavor to sustain an activist stance toward people-forest environment relations in the eastern United States. The approach will emphasize understanding and awareness rather than how-to-do-it specific guidelines. Rules-of-thumb can be quite misleading except when used by a professional well versed in the complex ecological, social, and economic factors involved in woodland management. The book will provide a rather simplified discussion of most aspects of the forest environment from the standpoint of the landowner and his community. It is written for laymen — those who are not foresters or ecologists but who have a deep interest in their woodland and its contribution to the community. The objective is to present useful concepts rather than technical details and to provide the information essential to an awareness of "environmental forestry" as related to your woodland. For more specific information landowners should consult professional foresters and technical references (see Appendix C).

The material in this book applies primarily to the eastern United States from the Great Plains to the Atlantic Ocean. The forests are predominantly of deciduous (hardwood) species except in the extreme North and in the deep South, where conifers are an important component of the forests. In the eastern United States about three-fourths of all forest lands are in small private ownership, and this book is addressed to those owners.

The book is structured to give pertinent background concepts on the ecological, economic, and social considerations of woodland management and ownership. Then each of the chief woodland values — timber, wildlife, recreation and aesthetics, and watershed — are discussed separately. But such values need not be considered separately, and Chapter 9 provides some concepts of harmonious and integrated uses combining the principles and ideas related in the previous chapters. Following this is a discussion of ownership matters, including protection of your forest property, especially as related to community pressures of all kinds. A bit of philosophy, including a scenario of future forests, a reminiscence of boyhood in the Catskills, and tactics for a better forest environment, concludes the book.

I would have had neither the motivation nor the knowledge to write this book except for the twenty years' experience of actual application of silviculture and forest management on many forest areas on the Kaskaskia Experimental Forest in southern Illinois. For that I am grateful to the United States Forest Service, my employer at that time. I am also grateful to Virginia Polytechnic Institute and State University and to the State University of New York College of Environmental Science and Forestry for providing the opportunity for me to work on this book. In addition, several colleagues in both institutions have reviewed chapters and given helpful comments. I especially want to recognize the artist, Mr. Francis Davis, who labored patiently with me to illustrate forest cultural practices clearly and accurately. Finally, I want to thank the several typists who copied and recopied the manuscript and my wife, Edith, for a good deal of forbearance.

Syracuse, New York   Leon S. Minckler
Fall 1974

Foreword

The overriding challenge in the world today is to build a life of quality, a life that offers opportunity and something of grace for all. In America, this future life is not one based on machines and buildings and gadgets, but on human dignity and individual worth.

The crux of the challenge is this: To provide the chance for our 212 million Americans to lead decent, productive lives while, at the same time, we prepare this land — this society — for 100 million more Americans within the next quarter-century.

The crisis of our cities, perhaps the most serious to face us as a people, has its roots in our failure to plan for change. We have failed to develop public and private institutions and policies that would shape and control the unprecedented technological and productive forces that have been unleashed over the past fifty years.

Since the end of World War II, the beginning of the so-called Nuclear Era, more than twenty million Americans moved from the countryside to the city. A third of our total population left the cities and settled in suburbia. In that same period, three million farms disappeared in the technological revolution that swept — and is still sweeping — through the U.S. agricultural sector.

All of this, and more, occurred without any real national recognition of what it meant. More than 140 million Americans, seven out of every ten, are crowded on just 2 percent of the land. This massive concentration and dislocation of people has created unfathomable stresses and strains on our homes, our governments, our schools and churches, and our neighborhoods. We have seen the results of this unthinking people-space equation exploding on our television screens and in the newspapers — the quantum leaps in crime, delinquency, drugs, and welfare.

Many of us who live in or represent rural states — my native state of West Virginia is the second most rural state in America in terms of population dispersal — have seen the other side of the resulting mass exodus from the farms and small towns. If through lack of national planning we permit our small towns and rural areas to grow to weeds, if by failure to act we continue to force the further abandonment of small-town America, we are feeding the fires that are stirring the once-great inner cities and the erosion that blights so many of our suburban communities.

If present trends continue for the next quarter-century, one hundred million additional Americans will be piled on top of the angry and frustrated millions already in our major metropolises. And more and more of our natural resources will be exploited and wasted to fuel the concentrated, and politically potent, demands for short-term survival of massed populations.

There are indications of a growing movement across the country to meet these developing problems. In our search for serenity, for surcease from the mounting tensions of day-to-day living, there is a swelling clamor for conservation, for preservation, and a return to the slower pace of yesteryear.

Concern and nostalgia are not enough. We must harness these emerging forces within a national framework and a coordinated effort, or we will repeat the mistakes of the past.

We have in this nation the resources to do what we will. No one questions our ability to go to the moon, or to orbit crews around this planet. Why, then, question whether we can build a decent environment here on Earth? There is no good reason why we cannot create a national plan for desirable geographic distribution of economic opportunity, to give all Americans the institutional system needed to develop and monitor a continually evolving balanced national growth and development plan.

One of the major issues of the 93rd Congress involved the federal government's role in land-use planning. Legislation was introduced, and hotly debated, that would establish a national land-use policy and would authorize the Secretary of Interior to make grants to assist the states to develop and implement state land-use programs. Still unresolved is how to effect such a national plan without directly involving private interests. As written, the pending legislation would provide for coordination of federal programs and policies which have a land-use impact and further coordinate planning and management of adjacent non-federal lands.

Dr. Leon S. Minckler is a knowledgeable and dedicated professional. He has given meaningful testimony before our Subcommittee on Public Lands on the issue of National Forest Management and has counseled with me on numerous occasions regarding the complex questions involving proper forest management.

Author-educator Leon Minckler has provided a substantial contribution to our store of knowledge about land-use management. Our forests and woodlands constitute a vital part of the total ecosystem which must be nurtured in future years. His call to action by individual small forest owners for systematic and long-range conservation is reinforced by meticulously researched methods of practical application. To the 4.5 million private forest landowners of America, his book should become a valuable reference for improving the quality of our environment and realizing the potential productivity of our forest lands.

As the most intelligent species on Earth, Man can certainly provide for himself — and yet prudently protect the total ecosystem from unnecessary and unacceptable degradation. Our abiding confidence in man's good judgment and action is expressed well by poet James Russell Lowell, who wrote:

New times demand new measures, and new men;
The world advances, and in time outgrows
The laws that in our father's day were best;
And doubtless, after us some better scheme
Will be shaped out by wiser men than we,
Made wiser by the steady growth of truth.

Professor Minckler has given us a significant package of truth, presented in lucid fashion, which should prove beneficial to the environmentalist and industrialist alike.

November 1974   Jennings Randolph
                                 United States Senator, West Virginia

Contents

1   A Call to Action   1
     A Concept of Conservation   3
     The Woodland Forests   4
     Objectives of Woodland Owners   5
     Values from Woodland Management   6
     The Importance of Small Woodland Ownership   7
     Geographic Scope   9

2   Ecology of Woodland Culture   11
     Ecological Principles   12
     Eastern Forests   14
          Appalachian Mixed Hardwood Forest   17
          Oak-Hickory Forest   17
          Oak-Pine Forest   18
          Northern Hardwood Forest   18
          Bottomland Hardwood Forest   18
          Northern Coniferous Forest   19
          Southeastern Coniferous Forest   19
     Species Ecology   21
     Woodland Silvics   24
     Controlling the Character of the Forest   27
     The Concept of Sustained Yield   32
     Integrated and Multiple Uses   32
     Putting It All Together   34

3   The Economics of Small Woodlands   35
     The Meaning of Woodland Economics   36
     Timber as a By-Product   37
     The Economics of Integrated Use   42

4	Social Values of Forest Environments	45
	Forests and Human Behavior	45
	Direct Social Benefits of Forests	47
5	Timber Production	51
	Tree Classes	52
	Application of Tree Classes	59
	Maintaining Forest Growing Stock	61
	Natural Regeneration	61
	Choosing a Method of Regeneration Cutting	68
	Single Tree Selection	69
	Group Selection	69
	Shelterwood	70
	Seed Tree	70
	Clearcutting	70
	Yield of Timber	72
	Regulation of Woodlands	75
	Planting Trees for Timber Production	76
6	Wildlife and Fish Habitat	79
	Wildlife Habitat Management	81
	Habitat Requirements	
	of Some Common Game Species	83
	Whitetail Deer	83
	Ruffed Grouse	86
	Wild Turkey	88
	Tree Squirrels	88
	Beaver	90
	Miscellaneous Species	90
	Pond Management for Fish	92
	The Future of Wildlife	94
7	Recreation and Aesthetics	99
	Recreation in the Forest Environment	99
	Maintaining Open Wild Fields	104
	Aesthetics in the Forest Environment	106
8	Protection of Watershed Values	111
	Watershed Protection	112
	Water Yield	116

	Water Quality	117
9	Harmonious and Integrated Uses	119
	Guide for Integrated Uses	120
	Species Composition	120
	Regeneration	120
	Growth Rate of Trees	122
	Forest Diversity	122
	Forest Density	122
	Tree Quality or Condition	123
	Silvicultural Systems	123
	Effects of Intermediate Cutting	123
	Logging Methods	123
	Sustained Yield	124
	Costs and Values	124
	Small Ownerships	124
	Harmony of Wildlife, Recreation, and Aesthetics	124
	Integration of Timber Values	128
	Integrating Watershed and Water Values	134
	Integrated Use in the Sample Woodland	135
10	Protecting Your Forest Property	139
	Control of Damaging Agents	140
	Steps in Forest Protection	147
	Your Damaged Woodland — An Example	148
11	The Challenge of Woodland Ownership	155
	What Is a Good Buy?	156
	Diversity of Forests and Topography	157
	Costs and Opportunity	157
	Future Developments	157
	Presence of Streams or Lakes	157
	Accessibility	158
	Productivity	158
	Forest Condition and Past Treatment	159
	Markets for Goods and Services	159
	Social Services and Conveniences	159
	Presence of Buildings	159
	Size of Ownership	160

	Financial and Legal Considerations	160
	Woodland Management Policy	163
12	Forests of the Future	165
	Recollections of Childhood	166
	Scenario I — Man vs. Nature	170
	Scenario II — Man with Nature	172
	Forest Ecotactics	175
Appendixes		183
A	Assistance to Woodland Owners	183
	State Forestry Conservation Departments	188
	U.S.D.A. Cooperative Extension Services, Extension Foresters	190
	U.S.D.A. Soil Conservation Service State Offices	192
	State Fish and Game Departments	193
B	Sample Timber Sale Contract	197
C	Helpful References	201
	Ecology and Conservation	201
	Woodland Management	206
	Woodland Silviculture	212
	Wildlife and Fish Management	215
	Landscape, Aesthetics, and Recreation	218
	Urbanized Country Environment	221
Index		225

List of Tables

Table 2.1	Species Characteristics	30
Table 3.1	Summary of Results on 21-Acre Poor Woodland	43
Table 3.2	Timber Costs and Returns	44
Table 5.1	Expected Growth Rates	78

WOODLAND ECOLOGY

1

A Call to Action

TUCKED AWAY in a remote corner of the Milky Way, lost in the vastness of the Universe, spins a tiny speck of matter inhabited by Man, a self-designated supreme being. From a few hundred thousand miles this Earth appears as a blue and white mottled sphere with touches of brown and green. It is the home of a vast array of living creatures and plants; it is unique and it is beautiful. Man now threatens to slowly destroy this beauty and this life.

Earth has a combination of utterly fantastic and most improbable characteristics. Fresh clear water falls on the Earth's surface to sustain life and provide beauty in clouds, rivers, and oceans. An Earth star, the Sun, is just far enough away to provide warmth and energy without burning. The solid core of Earth is enclosed in an envelope of atmosphere which protects and sustains life and makes possible the breezes, the red sunsets, and the glorious smell and feel of the soft spring air.

Added to all these wonders is another most improbable wonder. The Earth is tipped on its axis in relation to the Sun just enough to provide spring, summer, fall, and winter seasons on its surface. This makes possible the diversity and the complexity of the Earth that we call home.

This is truly a unique Earth. The exact combination of circumstances which have occurred over the last four and a half billion years has happened nowhere else, though similar events have probably occurred elsewhere in the Universe. Man's prototype as an erect being appeared about twenty-five million years ago, and Man as a thinking animal probably appeared two million years ago. What has this thinking animal done to his Earth in the last few hundred years?

The answer can be direct and simple, though the solutions and implications are exceedingly complex. Through his domination and destruction of other natural life and its environment, through exploding population, through misplaced technology, through increased consumption and waste, and through needless and selfish materialism, Man is now wasting and polluting his own home. Other species have been reduced or eliminated, and, without a change of direction, Man himself will be diminished or destroyed by his own waste and violence. It is no longer fun or even safe to swim in most of our rivers, breathe the air in most big cities, or walk on a spring evening in a city park; and beautiful woodlands near urban areas are more and more scarce.

We can blame Man, not Nature. Except in a cosmological sense Nature maintains a steady state, resources are cycled and used again and again, and the environment is essentially unchanged over very long periods of time. Man destroys resources, or causes lengthening of the return cycle. The environment is polluted with smog, DDT, industrial waste, sewage, radioactive material, and various other wastes. Excess carbon dioxide in the atmosphere, or garbage and trash in our waters may ultimately be recycled but only in geologic time and too late for use by our species. In the meantime, we live and breathe polluted air and picnic in a degraded forest by a polluted stream. Great lakes die from pollution, DDT is found in Antarctic penguins, and the American eagle is vanishing. Noise pollution and crowding are pressing in on a generation already hypertense. There is no hiding place. We must take action to save our Earth of life and beauty, and we must do it soon.

"Soon" is not quite too late. We can still save much of the beauty and usefulness of forests, wildlife, and waters so characteristic of this Earth. Judged by past experience, however, Man will wait until his back is against the wall. We can then have an ant hill society, but we will not have joyous life in a world of beauty and freedom. The younger generations and all concerned people will have to make the choice and take the action. We must choose a new life style toward fulfillment of the spirit and the mind and away from dominant materialism. We must choose fewer people, less affluence, and less fierce competition for material advantages between people and nations. We may decide that the essential humanity of Man can live in harmony with Nature on this Earth.

But there are grave obstacles and pitfalls to overcome inherent in the very nature of Man. Loren Eiseley expressed it well in *The Immense Journey:*

> The need is not really for more brains, the need is now for a gentler, a more tolerant people than those who won for us against the ice, the tiger, and the bear. The hand that hefted the ax, out of some old blind allegiance to the past, fondles the machine gun as lovingly. It is a habit man will have to break to survive, but the roots go very deep.

We must understand that the old methods no longer work in this present world. If we fight for ever-increasing material abundance we will destroy our uniquely beautiful environment and, eventually, our species. The choice is ours. The goal is vital. With total dedication the attainment is barely possible.

Are there any solutions? Yes, but the solutions involve a sharp turnabout in our values, directions, and goals — even in the management of our woodlands, which will be discussed in this book. In addition, we must have a turnabout in our political life. This involves effective governance through democratic processes implemented by dedicated people and leaders. Also, there must be an industrial revolution that will *recycle* resources; not merely speed them on a one-way road to the ocean, the atmosphere, or a junk pile.

Is there some concept that will put us on the road to a solution of environmental problems? The concept has been touched on, but some thoughts from Aldous Huxley provide reinforcement. Huxley says we must shift our attention from the merely political to the basic biological aspects of the human condition and the natural resources which support us. He says that good, realistic politics should work for the benefit and fulfillment of the human species as a whole. Bad, unrealistic politics promotes idolatrous nationalism in the context of population explosion, missiles, atomic warheads, pollution, and wasted and poorly used resources. What Huxley means can be expressed by the modern concept of "conservation."

A CONCEPT OF CONSERVATION

The utility of the concept of conservation is the application of knowledge (and goodwill) to insure a safe and happy journey for Man on the spaceship Earth. This implies certain goals: that we attain a reasonably limited population and choose a humanistic society with concern for future generations and humility toward Nature. The concept embodies continued preservation of environmental quality, harmony between Man's needs and Nature's laws, and environmental management to perpetuate reasonably high living standards and aesthetic, spiritual, and recreational values. It also recognizes that these goals are often circumscribed by economic and political limitations which must also be somehow managed. It is necessary to apply the science and concepts of ecology, total environmental and social wisdom, to attain these goals.

Forest conservation is but a piece of the whole — a piece cut from the same cloth. The details of ecological management of forests are different, but the basic approach is the same as for the total environment. Forests cannot be properly managed except through a holistic approach which considers all the known scientific factors and human values. This is the approach that should be taken to your woodland.

THE WOODLAND FORESTS

Ecologists consider a forest to be an ecosystem. The word *ecology* is derived from the Greek word *ekos* meaning *household*. A forest is a household of trees and other plants growing together. The word *ecosystem* refers to the interacting system of plants, animals, micro-organisms, soil, and climate. Foresters (forest ecologists) try to understand this system, to learn how to modify it for Man's needs, and to keep it healthy while being used, observed, or enjoyed. A forester should have a certain reverence for the forest community to serve fully and well in his or her profession.

Forests of the eastern United States constitute one of the most complex plant associations in the world. Many species, ages, and types occur in a geographic setting of streams, lakes, and diversified topography, intimately mixed and varied from acre to acre. Rainfall ranges from adequate to superabundant, and temperatures vary widely. Forests range from tropical hardwoods in Florida to boreal conifers in Maine and from the oak-pine forests of Long Island to the alpine vegetation of Mt. Marcy. In addition, and within the same latitude and altitude, site and soil differences are very great in magnitude. Trees may grow only thirty feet tall on dry ridgetops, while three hundred feet down the slope they may be a hundred or more feet in height.

The woodland forests of the eastern United States constitute the major portion of the open-space landscape. Without forests the countryside would be desolate and naked and no fit habitation for Man. The environmental and humanistic values of forests are discussed in detail in this book, but it should be clear from the outset that forests are essential to a high-quality environment, that their existence is not negotiable.

OBJECTIVES OF WOODLAND OWNERS

What you, the landowner, actually do in the forest depends on your objectives, assuming the objectives are compatible with the forest, site, and climatic conditions. This is a key point and must be observed in any forestry program. Forests may be desired for timber, for wildlife, or for aesthetics; or the objective may be a combination of these and other uses. The silvicultural treatments may be different for different objectives. For example, a forest of trees the same age and species would generally be unfavorable for aesthetics and wildlife. A forest kept as low sprouts would be good for deer browsing but useless for timber, recreation, and aesthetics. Fortunately, there are happy combinations of uses and these integrated uses are commonly the most desirable for you and will be discussed in Chapter 9 at some length.

Owners' objectives are so important that another point should be made. A forester, public or private, who fails to determine your objectives, or blandly assumes he knows best what the proper objectives are, should be dismissed! However, you should discuss *alternatives* with the forester and determine whether or not your objectives are harmonious with the ecological conditions of the forest and perhaps the social conditions in your community.

In general, what practices are possible in a forest ownership in order to attain various objectives? The manipulation of the forest environment is usually called *silviculture*. This is the art of applied ecology within some economic or other limits. It includes the regeneration of tree seedlings and their tending and manipulation over a long period to produce the desired forest. Successful application of silviculture requires a knowledge of the necessary growth conditions and the complex interaction within the forest eco- system. For example, hemlock will develop under the shade of other trees, while yellow-poplar must have at least half of full sun- light from the start. Black walnut will not develop on a dry, shal- low soil, but post oak will live and grow there. Logging and cutting practices on steep slopes with shallow soils should be different than on gentle slopes with deep soils. An earth dam cannot be con- structed in gravelly soils unless clay is added; and soil fertility affects the kind and quantity of wildlife present. These brief exam- ples illustrate some of the ecological information which can be applied in managing a forest property. The landowner-manager must accumulate a rather large bag of tricks or seek competent professional help. It is hoped that this book will give the con- cerned woodland owner some understanding of the problems and their solution.

VALUES FROM WOODLAND MANAGEMENT

What values, then, can be realized from the managed forest com- munity and why are they important? Personal satisfaction and pleasure will constitute a large portion of the motivation for management. In this case self-interest reinforces the environmental and social benefits to the community, if not obtained at the ex- pense of a healthy forest environment. For example, a healthy and diversified forest, with good wildlife food and habitat, would be an asset to the whole community, especially if like-minded land- owners in the area followed similar aims. This could be done in combination with correctly executed timber cutting which would benefit the community as well as the owners. If, however, a large portion of the forests in the community were clearcut, the range of appeal to wildlife would be greatly narrowed, the timber base would be reduced for decades, the value of the forests for recrea- tion and aesthetics could be greatly diminished, and mineral and silt pollution of streams and lakes would be accelerated. What you do on your woodland affects both you and your community. This is the main justification for the conservation subsidies which are available from the federal government.

You will find almost without exception that several integrated uses on your woodland will return more total value in combined satisfaction and money than any one use. Besides, good management for one use often enhances other values. The use of forests for timber value alone, so prevalent in past forestry practice, is not the answer for small woodland owners, and this book will tell you why.

In most of the eastern United States it is only a short step from a rural community to some urban area. Are city people interested in your forest? Yes, they are. In fact, sometimes they are a downright nuisance, but mutually beneficial arrangements can be made. Environmental values concerned with air, water, and scenery can be enjoyed by urbanites without sacrifice from you or your own community. Hunting, fishing, hiking, and other forms of recreation require some kind of understanding and perhaps compensation to the landowner — about which more later. But the whole nation, and especially the cities, benefits from good management of your forest environment. You may justly deserve something more substantial than a verbal "thank you."

THE IMPORTANCE OF SMALL WOODLAND OWNERSHIP

Do you have the impression that small private forest ownership is "small potatoes" in this great country of ours? If so, you are wrong. According to the United States Forest Service, 59 percent of the potentially productive forest land — 300 million acres — is owned by private nonindustrial owners. In the eastern part of the country the proportion of forest land owned by private non-industrial owners is much higher, about 73 percent. In the Northeast, including the Lake States, 56 percent of this forest land is owned by non-farmers such as teachers, doctors, lawyers, businessmen, hunting clubs, and just plain citizens who love the outdoors.

There are 4.5 million private-forest landowners in this country; the average holding is small, but in total such owners control 38 percent of the commercial timber volume. The small woodland owner, without knowing it, controls a major portion of both timber supply and environmental values from the forest. It is time the people of the local communities and in the cities interspersed in the eastern woodlands realized this fact and started a true partnership to raise the quality of the environment and obtain all the potential values from the forest. It is also time the forests of this country made their full contribution to the safety and beauty of our Earth.

Countryside of woodlands and open farm land in a typical pattern in eastern United States: fields occupy the more level valley land and the gentler lower slopes where soils are deeper; woodlands occupy the steeper slopes and ridges.

GEOGRAPHIC SCOPE

This book will discuss forest environmental thinking, or environmental forestry, for the hardwood types of the eastern United States from the Plains to the Atlantic Ocean and from the Great Lakes to the piney woods of the deep South. The actual forest types in the eastern United States are described and mapped in the next chapter. Although some of the general principles apply to the coniferous types in the extreme North and South, the thrust of the discussion and recommendations apply to the hardwood types in the Appalachian, Northeast, Central, and Lake States regions. This is where small woodlands are most heavily concentrated and where the juxtaposition of people and forests is most intimate. This is also where the concerted action of people can bring more recognition of forest environmental problems and action for their solution.

2

Ecology of Woodland Culture

AN'S UNDERSTANDING of Nature is imperfect at best. We can see the outward direct causes and effects, but Nature's deeper and more complex relationships are often a mystery and will remain so for a very long time. If we approach these mysteries with humility, we are in the right frame of mind to seek relationships that will be helpful in practical matters, such as managing a forest. Ecology is in part an attitude of mind and a mode of action. An ecologist knows that relationships exist in Nature, and so by seeking he finds them where others would fail. In the past, simple ecological knowledge has often been neglected by foresters who have been bemused by the day-to-day routine aspects of their profession. Ecology is still a science of considerable mystery, but we have not yet practiced what we do know or what is available to know. You and I can do wonders with a little ecology, and the intellectual attitude is as important as the facts.

The practice of silviculture, or applied ecology, means that the silviculturist starts with a knowledge of how the forest community and its component parts behave in a particular environment. The silviculturist then applies this knowledge in the culture or manipulation of forests to attain certain objectives. The forest owner has a vital interest in why and how this is done and what can be accomplished.

11

ECOLOGICAL PRINCIPLES

Ecology is the science of the interrelatedness of living organisms to their environment and to each other. In a forest or woodland the trees are vitally influenced by the climate, topography, and the soil. They also react sharply to each other and to other plant and animal life. A forest is a whole. I will discuss very briefly the general and well-known ecological principles especially applicable to woodlands.

In simple terms the forest ecological factors can be grouped into five classes: (1) the physical environment, (2) tree species characteristics, (3) interrelations among trees and other plants, (4) interrelations with animals, and (5) natural succession. All of these factors are closely intertwined, and, like a spider web, it is impossible to alter one strand without changing some of the others. I will explain the ecological items in each of the five groups and illustrate the concepts by examples and further discussion later in this chapter.

The forest physical environment includes the climate, topography and soil. Directly affecting forest trees are sunlight, warmth, soil moisture, soil physical characteristics, and soil nutrients. Through geologic time forest species have become adapted to the combinations of physical factors where they now occur naturally. Climate is the overall pattern of seasonal temperature and precipitation and determines the general forest type or the species present. The soil complex, including micro-organisms, determines the size and growth rate of trees, and to some extent the species present. The soil complex is determined chiefly by the underlying rock material, the topography, the drainage patterns, and finally by the forest itself. The chief ecological lesson here is that tree species and forest types should be encouraged only under the climatic and soil conditions to which they are adapted.

The more important tree species characteristics are seeding and germination habits, growth rate and pattern of growth, tolerance to shade, reaction to soil physical condition, tree form and branching habits, space requirements and response to release from competition with other trees, length of life and size at maturity, resistance to damaging agents such as diseases and weather, interrelations with wildlife, and the variable inherent characteristics of individuals within a given tree species. A simplified lesson is that the forester or manager should understand the species characteristics before starting to cut, treat, or otherwise manipulate the forest. Everything is connected to everything else.

The interrelation among trees is concerned chiefly with competition for space — that is, a place to grow where adequate sunlight, soil moisture, and nutrients can be obtained. This factor is connected closely to species requirements and tolerance as already discussed. All these interacting forces determine the density, species composition, size, and age arrangement of trees as they intermingle in the forest. In managing woodlands foresters pay considerable attention to controlling the forest characteristics outlined above. If done within the limits of the ecological factors discussed here, forests can be altered to some degree and certain values may be enhanced.

The interrelations between forests and animal life are not so obvious, but they are real and in some cases can be critical. It is well known, for example, that squirrels and birds disseminate tree seed. A forest as a habitat can be altered or greatly damaged by overuse from animals, deer in particular. Under natural conditions the forest as a habitat is reasonably balanced with animal populations. But when Man eliminates all deer predators, for example, the balance is drastically upset and deer populations may explode. The same thing happens after extensive heavy forest cuttings which produce an abnormal amount of browse food over a wide area. The habitat-animal balance should be maintained, and both the animal population and the habitat should be managed.

Micro-organisms and fungi are an inherent component of forest soils, contributing to fertility and to the breakdown of raw organic matter into soil material. Any drastic forest disturbance usually changes the soil and the soil micro-plant and animal life at least temporarily. This in turn has an effect on fertility until more optimum conditions are restored. The forest, above and below ground level, is an integrated whole.

Natural succession of vegetation is what happens in nature over the years on bare ground such as an abandoned cultivated field, a fire-denuded area, or even a bare rock. The nature of this ecological succession is determined by the climate, the remaining soil mantle, and any residual vegetation. For example, forests gradually progress over many years through pioneer species such as aspen, fire cherry, and pine to species such as maple, beech, yellow birch, hemlock, spruce, oak, and hickory. This succession takes place because the pioneer species are much better adapted to the bare soil conditions, but their presence changes the site conditions so that the more permanent species can thrive and occupy the site. It is difficult to maintain pioneer species for long periods of time, though this is being done in some kinds of monoculture timber tree farming. The lesson for small woodland owners interested in both timber and non-timber uses is to follow, not oppose, the current of succession. At the same time it is possible to create local conditions favorable to maintaining some desired pioneer species such as aspen and white birch which are beneficial to wild-life and which have aesthetic appeal. Obviously it is necessary to know the species requirements, which will be discussed below.

EASTERN FORESTS

Eastern hardwood (deciduous) types in the United States extend from the Great Plains to the Atlantic Ocean and from the Gulf of Mexico to Canada. These forest types are interspersed with pine forests in the deep South and Southeast and pine and spruce forests in northern New England and the Lake States. There are several general types of hardwood forests in the eastern region, and they can be divided into two groups — the pioneer types such as fire cherry, aspen, and cottonwood which follow major disturb-ance, and the climax or sub-climax types which are more or less permanent occupants of a particular site in a particular climate.

Pioneer types are characteristically of one species, with trees of about the same age. They may quickly occupy a site after some severely destructive action such as land clearing, fire, disease, insect attack, floods, and in some cases clearcutting. Pioneer types are temporary and, if left alone, will convert naturally to the more stable hardwood types. Some species are intermediate or transi-tional in nature. Species like shortleaf pine, yellow-poplar, and white pine often invade disturbed areas but also form a part of the later mixed forests. These species often have high timber value and may be favored by foresters.

General forest types of the eastern United States are determined by the over-all climate. Local variations are related to local soil conditions: Oak-hickory, Oak-pine, Northern hardwoods, Northern coniferous, Appalachian mixed hardwoods, Southeastern coniferous, and Bottomland hardwoods.

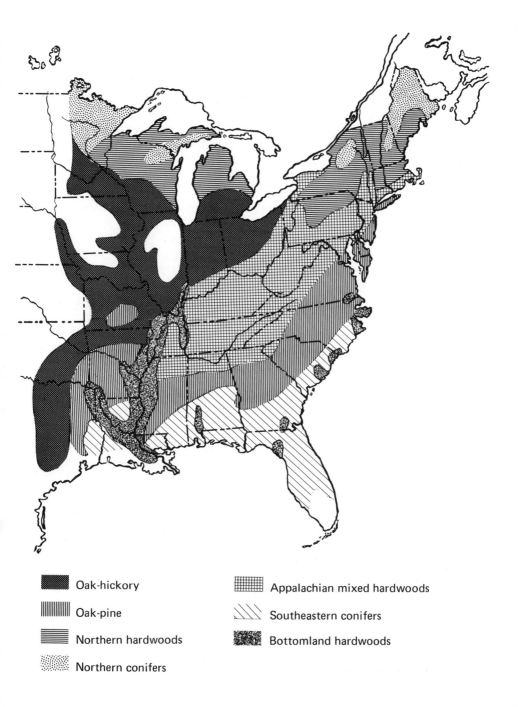

Oak-hickory

Oak-pine

Northern hardwoods

Northern conifers

Appalachian mixed hardwoods

Southeastern conifers

Bottomland hardwoods

All the later ecological stages of hardwood forests have certain characteristics in common: (1) they contain many species mixed together; (2) the tree ages are different, with age distribution by single trees or in small groups; and (3) the forest community is relatively stable in relation to internal changes and response to climatic and site factors.

In the eastern region of the United States, the overall forest type can be related to the climate. But within climatic types the site — soil and topography — varies over a magnitude of several hundred percent. Thus, there are general types, each with great variations in species and biomass (total mass of all living plants) from acre to acre. This adds up to the great diversity so common to the eastern hardwood types.

The most complex forests, with the richest mixture of species, occur where the climate and soil are most favorable to tree growth. In the eastern United States this area covers West Virginia, southwestern Pennsylvania, southeastern Ohio, and a strip across eastern Kentucky and Tennessee and into northeastern Alabama. Adjacent to this central area on both the east and the west, precipitation is lower and the forests are somewhat simpler, although still complex. These combined regions, extending from New York to Alabama and from the Mississippi River to just east of the Blue Ridge, contain the *Appalachian Mixed Hardwood Forest.*

The midland area to the west and northwest, including the central states of Ohio, Indiana, Illinois, Missouri, and parts of Arkansas, Oklahoma, and Texas, is considerably drier than the Appalachian area. This is sometimes called the midland hardwoods or the *Oak-Hickory Forest.* It can be regarded as a transition between the Appalachian region and the prairie on the west.

The Ozark region in Missouri and Arkansas, and the Piedmont region extending on the Piedmont Plateau from New Jersey to Texas, is also relatively dry compared to the Appalachian region and can be called the *Oak-Pine Forest.* This is a transition between Appalachian hardwoods and the hard pine forests of the Coastal Plain.

The *Northern Hardwood Forest* occurs in northern Pennsylvania, New York, New England, and in the Lake States. This is a complex forest but still simpler than those of the Appalachian region. The species are hardy to cold weather, and the forest is a transition between those of the Appalachians and the simpler coniferous forests to the north.

All the major river flood plains, especially the Delta region of the Mississippi, are characterized by deep, moist, alluvial soils which support a lush growth of bottomland tree species. In the aggregate these areas make up the *Bottomland Hardwood Forest* which generally has a high value for timber and very fast tree growth.

The remainder of the forest land in the East is occupied by the *Northern Coniferous Forest* in the extreme North and the *Southeastern Coniferous Forest* on the Atlantic and Gulf Coastal Plains. The former is a boreal forest of spruce, balsam, and pine, and the latter is composed almost entirely of southern or hard pines (see map of forest types).

The eastern United States has the greatest variety and diversity of forest types, sites, and conditions of any other temperate region in the world. It also has most of the people of the country and most of the rivers, streams, and lakes. It is truly a meeting place of forests, waters, mountains, and people.

It would be useful to characterize briefly each of the seven general forest types in terms of some distinctive or essential point. You can determine the fit of your own woodland, remembering that site and past history differences can be very great, even on a single woodland.

Appalachian Mixed Hardwood Forest

These forests have near-optimum growing conditions and the richest mixture of species on the widest variety of sites. The major species and species groups are red oaks, white oak, yellow-poplar, basswood, white ash, sugar maple, cucumber, beech, blackgum, hickories, buckeye, chestnut oak, butternut, elm, black locust, yellow birch, red maple, black walnut, dogwood, redbud, yellow-wood, and even silverbell. It is not uncommon to find fifteen to twenty species on a single acre. These forests have high value for timber but are especially useful for multiple and integrated uses.

Oak-Hickory Forest

Oaks are the key tree species. Both red and white oaks are mixed with some species of the Appalachian Forest, depending on the soil and site quality. On dry sites such as ridges and southerly slopes, or sites with thin soil, the species are few — chiefly white oak, post oak, scarlet oak, black oak, hickories, and locally black-gum and chestnut oak. Species mixtures on moist sites with deep soils are more complex, including northern red oak, yellow-poplar, black walnut, sugar maple, white ash, blackgum, beech, and dog-wood in addition to the other oaks and hickories. Yet nowhere in the upland midland area does forest complexity reach that of the Appalachian Forest. Precipitation is less, and the water balance as determined by the precipitation-evaporation ratio is less favorable to forest development.

Oak-Pine Forest

The key difference between this and the Oak-Hickory Forest is the presence of hard pines — shortleaf, Virginia, pitch, and lob-lolly — in more or less intimate mixture with the hardwoods. The oaks and hickories are the predominant hardwoods, and species of the Appalachian Forest such as yellow-poplar, black walnut, and white ash occur only on the moist sites with deep soils. A combination of hot temperatures and poor sites is associated with the occurrence of pines in these forests.

Northern Hardwood Forest

This is a cold-climate forest characterized by beech, birch, maple, and hemlock, usually in intimate mixture and of all ages. Yellow birch is the key birch, but sweet, paper, and gray birch are also common. Sugar maple is most characteristic, but red maple also occurs. Paper and gray birch, aspen, and red maple are more likely to occur as pioneer species in disturbed areas. Other species occasionally occurring in the climax forest are black cherry, white ash, white pine, and spruce, usually as scattered individuals or small groups. This type occurs only at high latitudes (see map) or at elevations between about 3,000 and 5,000 feet in the Appalachian Forest.

Bottomland Hardwood Forest

This is a unique type existing on areas of transported soil and water. Soils are alluvial, and water supply to the forest consists of runoff from the adjacent uplands as well as the current precipitation. Forests are complex and lush with many species of trees which grow to a large size. One small virgin forest on the Mississippi flood plain in Missouri had thirty tree species ranging in size from one to forty-nine inches in diameter. New alluvial lands along rivers nearly always are pioneered by eastern cottonwood and willow. Later, a large number of different species invade the areas as they become more stabilized. The more important of these species are sweetgum, elms, hackberry, sycamore, honeylocust, box elder, blackgum, water tupelo, white oaks, red oaks, red maple, silver maple, hickories, and cypress. The species mixtures are rather closely related to the wetness and drainage of the site. Cypress and water tupelo occupy sites with the poorest drainage; cottonwood, sycamore, and sweetgum grow well only on well-drained sites.

Northern Coniferous Forest

This is essentially a spruce-fir forest of the far northeastern United States in New England and the Lake States and the higher elevations in the Adirondacks. It also tends to occur on poorly drained areas in the Northern Hardwood Forest. Pines also make up part of this coniferous type and occur on the well-drained sandy areas in the Lake States, New York, and New England. White pine tends to be mixed with hardwoods on better sandy sites, but red pine and jack pine often occur as pure stands on sandy soils. Throughout the northern United States these pines, along with aspen and fire cherry, are widespread pioneers after land abandonment or logging and fire. Much of the Lake States and New England are now occupied by these pioneer forest types.

Southeastern Coniferous Forest

This is a forest of hard pines in a hot climate and on chiefly sandy soils. Rainfall is heavy, but because of the soil and climate, sites are relatively dry for tree growth. The area has traditionally been subject to frequent and severe burns. Much of the original forest was longleaf pine, but most of this has been destroyed by logging and the present forest is mostly loblolly and slash pine with some mixture of shortleaf pine and remnants of longleaf pine in the Coastal Plain and Carolina Sand Hill country. This coniferous forest is the "timber basket" of the South.

Yellow-poplar and oak saplings in a one-fifth-acre opening fifteen years after cutting mature and low quality trees. The light in this opening was about 60 percent of full sunlight and sufficient for good growth of young trees.

SPECIES ECOLOGY

If you know how tree species relate to the total environment you have taken the first essential step in understanding a forest and how to manage it for desired objectives. Foresters call this information the silvics or silvical characteristics of forest trees. It is a part of the whole picture of the forest ecosystem. The foresters' use of the term "silvics" is mostly for professional convenience. Silvics cannot be fully treated in this book, but the References in Appendix C provide bits of useful information for some of the more common tree species.

Tree species occur naturally and grow well within a certain range of temperature and precipitation conditions — that is, the climate. In technical terms, this is the *range* of the species. The range border is not a sharp line, but as climatic conditions become more unfavorable the tree can no longer compete with other plant species and gradually disappears. Climatic ranges are related to latitude, altitude, and the rainfall amounts and distribution. It is almost axiomatic that the best results from management happen when the species concerned are well within their natural range.

Next to climate the most important factor determining species occurrence and success is *site* quality. It is by far the most important local factor affecting the forest. The site quality is the sum of soil and topographic features of a particular place for growth of a particular species. Site conditions include the factors of soil type, soil depth, aspect, slope steepness, topographic position, and soil drainage. Well-drained and aerated deep soils on lower north-facing aspects or in bottomlands are the most productive in terms of both growth and forest diversity. Dry thin soils on exposed ridges or south-facing slopes are least productive. Site quality relates strongly to species present, growth rate, total biomass, timber quality, and forest diversity. Silviculture is unthinkable without due consideration of site quality.

Other silvical factors which vary by species are type and time of flowering, time of seeding and amount and dissemination of seed, requirements and limitations for germination and regeneration, shape of crown and branching habits, hardiness to cold, and ability to sprout.

Next to species range and site requirements, the third most important silvical factor is what foresters call *tolerance.* This is the ability of the tree species to grow in reduced light produced by

Yellow-poplar saplings in a small forest opening on a good cove site nineteen years after the overstory was removed. Dominant saplings are free to grow and are nearly half the height of adjacent large trees of the uncut forest shown in the background.

Mixed oak and hickory saplings fifteen years after the seedlings on the ground were released from overhead shade. This group of saplings is well on its way to forming a new stand of trees.

the shade of other trees or non-woody plants. A knowledge of tolerance is central to silviculture because trees must grow together in competition with each other for light and for soil moisture and nutrients. Each species has its own ecological niche in a given climatic-site-light condition. For example, yellow-poplar outgrows all other species on well-drained but deep fertile soils where at least 50 percent of full sunlight is present. But in deep shade it cannot compete with sugar maple or hickory, and on dry ridges it cannot compete with oaks. The relationships are complex, but a working knowledge is available for use; experienced foresters or ecologists can usually make the right decisions, unless encumbered by prior commitments or by prejudice for certain methods.

The species that have persisted in the eastern hardwood forests since the ice ages have great resistance to damaging agents such as diseases, insects, and fire. The native mixed hardwood forests are remarkably permanent and stable. Diversity and adaptation to the climate and site and resistance to the endemic pathogens are the keys. Only the exotic diseases like chestnut blight and Dutch elm disease have taken a heavy toll. Thus beware of those who urge you to develop uniform forests or to plant exotic species.

By way of illustration, some of the more important silvical characteristics for some common tree species are summarized on Table 2.1. For full information see the reference for the silvics of forest trees in the Appendix.

WOODLAND SILVICS

An observing walk through your woods can reveal all sorts of interesting ecological insights. You may first notice the topography and then that the kind and height of trees are different in different places. Ridge tops and southerly-aspect slopes usually have thin, dry soils forested with dry-site species like oaks, hickory, and perhaps some pine. Mature trees are short, perhaps no taller than 50 feet. But walk toward the lower north-aspect slopes and find 90-to-100-foot trees of yellow-poplar, red oak, sugar maple, and birch. This is one of the most striking aspects of eastern forests: the site quality is so variable that forest diversity is guaranteed. Walk from the well-drained area and skirt along the edge of a swamp. The species will be completely different. The first northern white cedar (or other swamp species) may be less than ten feet from an upland oak or maple. The overall climate throughout the woodland is the same, but the soil and moisture conditions at the tree roots are profoundly different. (But remember that site variability is not so pronounced on flat uniform land.)

Look at the arrangement of the trees in the forest in terms of the amount of sunlight they receive. This is determined by the tolerance (to shade) of the species, and tolerance cannot be correctly judged except within a given forest type and region. In your woodland, sugar maple and other tolerant seedlings and saplings may be abundant under the shade of large trees, but you will not find thriving black cherry or yellow-poplar. These species, and many others, require at least 50 to 60 percent of full day-long sunlight. You will find them growing in forest openings, reaching toward the open sky. Even the tolerant species grow much faster in forest openings, and you will notice how these trees seem to "sneak" through little openings in the forest canopy.

Openings are vital to the regeneration of a hardwood forest. They provide a horizontal and vertical space where new trees can start and grow. This air space allows the entrance of sunlight, and the soil space (often forgotten) provides soil moisture and root room for young trees. Notice how trees growing directly in an opening are straight; they reach straight up. Hardwoods are phototrophic; they bend toward the light. You will observe some trees which lean and bend toward a source of light in the canopy. By proper cutting of openings a forester can create a forest of straighter trees.

Your walk in the woods can also reveal that trees can adapt to crowding, called *density* by foresters. Do you see trees growing close together, with long clean boles, and a crown length (distance from bottom of live crown to the top of the tree) only 30 percent of the total height? These trees are growing too close together and are small in diameter for their age. The other extreme is the lone tree with limbs nearly to the ground. Then you will see others with a 50 to 60 percent crown ratio. These trees have had about the right amount of growing space. Making openings for regeneration and regulating the growing space of trees are about the most important things you can do in your woodland. Both of these operations must be properly related to tolerance and site requirements. This is the practice of silviculture.

A typical unmanaged oak-hickory forest in the Midwest. The forest was partially cut about fifty to sixty years earlier, and the present forest is uneven-aged, containing many species and a wide range of tree qualities. The cove and lower north slope in the middle and background is a good site and contains yellow-poplar, northern red oak, and white oak. The right foreground shows a medium-dry south slope with black and scarlet oaks. This forest was later treated to eliminate or harvest the cull, low quality, and mature trees, thus providing openings for regeneration and a diversified forest more suitable for integrated uses.

CONTROLLING THE CHARACTER OF THE FOREST

The tree and shrub species which grow naturally in a healthy woodland are well adapted to the climate, soil, and site conditions, but within these limits the combinations of species can vary greatly. Species composition can be altered by (1) control of regeneration, (2) planting, (3) elimination of unwanted trees, and (4) favoring desired trees by releasing them from competition. Note, however, that there may be forces opposing your desires. This occurs when you wish to alter the natural trend, when weather conditions are unusual, when seed supply is scarce or super-abundant, or when wildlife is populated beyond the carrying capacity of the range.

How can ecological knowledge help in attaining desired species composition? An example will illustrate. Suppose you want a scattering of dogwood trees in your woodland. Dogwood is a slow-growing, small tree quite tolerant of overhead shade for growth and survival. However, it does not bloom well without strong sunlight for at least a portion of the day. It regenerates naturally quite well but is difficult to plant. It responds well to partial release from shade, and the release increases growth and blooming. The leaves are especially rich in mineral nutrients, and thus the presence of dogwood tends to recycle nutrients and enrich the forest topsoil. Dogwood grows well only on a fertile, moist, well-drained site and is an important component in the understory of eastern hardwood and coniferous forests. With this knowledge a forester, an ecologist, or even a careful layman could understand the possibilities for increasing the proportion of blooming dogwood in a woodland and devise forest treatments to accomplish it. Perhaps only the release of existing plants would be required.

Other species have different requirements and relations to the site and forest community. Most of the knowledge needed is available. The principles are the same, but the art of application differs for different situations. Characteristics of some of the more important forest species have already been given.

Trees in a forest may grow close together or far apart. Forest density affects the size and form of trees of a given species and age. The density, or competition among individuals in a forest community, can be rather easily regulated by the forestry practice called "thinning." You can have many smaller trees with narrow crowns or fewer large trees with large crowns or a combination.

Within wide limits of density the total wood volume growth and also the tree heights will be about the same. If the crown canopy is nearly closed the forest will fully utilize the sunlight, soil moisture, and nutrients available. Total growth, then, for a given species and age class, depends mostly on the site quality, that is, the capability of the soil-site and climatic complex.

An example will illustrate the application of knowledge about density to forest stands. To produce long straight boles for timber products, a rather high density during the sapling and pole stages would be required. The lower limbs would die from lack of sunlight and eventually drop off. For maximum wildlife food and shelter, some trees with long, wide crowns would be beneficial. Such trees produce greater quantities of seed (nuts), have larger limbs, provide a greater opportunity for wildlife dens, and are aesthetically pleasing because they add diversity of tree form.

After long periods without major disturbances, natural forests are usually uneven-aged, that is, the trees are of widely different ages. Forests arising after some major disturbance such as a killing fire, blow-down, or clearcutting are usually even-aged, at least for the first generation. Even-aged stands of jack pine or aspen follow logging and burning in the Lake States. As already discussed these are the pioneer species constituting an initial forest where the previous forest has been destroyed. Forests which have developed for several generations in response to climatic and soil-site factors tend to become uneven-aged and contain many species. They are more ecologically mature and stable than pioneer plant communities. For example, beech, birch, maple and hemlock develop at the lower elevations in the Adirondacks and mixed-oak and hickory in the uplands of the Central States.

But what Nature can do Man can, within limits, do more quickly if not better. Age differences in a forest add to the diversity of tree size and height. This may have advantages for sustained timber yield on a small forest, for wildlife and recreation, and for aesthetics. Age differences can be easily created by a cutting schedule and by cutting to assure successful regeneration of the harvested areas, whether openings are large or small. Clearcutting will result in an even-aged forest. Man can choose to emulate (but accelerate) the natural trend toward trees of different ages or he can produce a man-made major disturbance to obtain trees of the same age. Just how these operations are done will also have a profound effect on the species obtained by natural seeding.

Openings in the forest occur naturally through blow-downs, fire, and mortality of trees from various causes. Such openings are rather quickly filled with new growth of some kind, usually native species adapted to the site and shade conditions. In a managed forest, openings are created by cutting trees, usually for timber. These openings can be made to vary in size and number depending on the forest type and on the objectives of management. Openings are necessary for regeneration of new trees; they enhance food and habitat for wildlife, and as time goes on they add to the diversity and more natural appearance of the forest.

A forest opening, as the term is used here, means an opening large enough to allow tree reproduction and growth. In northern hardwood forests the removal of single large trees may be sufficient. In oak-hickory and mixed hardwood forests the openings should be larger, ranging all the way from one-eighth to a half-acre or so. This merges into clearcutting or patch cutting if the conditions and objectives warrant (see Chapter 5). The number of openings will depend on the number of trees and the volume cut. A light cut made frequently will result in fewer new openings at any one time and a larger number of age classes in the forest. A heavy cut made at longer intervals will result in more new openings and a smaller number of age classes. A clearcut forest necessarily results in one age class and very long intervals between harvests on that particular area.

Making openings in the forest by cutting is the forester's way of emulating Nature while at the same time harvesting the mature and unwanted low-quality trees. Furthermore, the forester can alter the forest and improve on Nature for his own purposes without violating ecological principles. This has large implications for integrated uses of forests and will be discussed in Chapter 9.

It has already been shown that the species, size, form, and age of trees in a forest can be strongly influenced by application of ecological principles. The health and condition of trees can also be influenced by silviculture. A healthy tree will be one naturally adapted to the site and climate, with adequate past and present growing space, and without past injury or serious disease. These conditions can be produced largely by the correct forest culture, including the elimination of poorer competing trees. Picturesque trees or trees with other desired features such as animal dens or nesting sites can be preserved. Given enough time such trees could even be produced by cultural methods, though this has not so far been done in forest practice.

Table 2.1

SPECIES CHARACTERISTICS

Relative tolerance*	Relative site requirements†	Soil drainage tolerated	Tree size	Relative growth rate	Regeneration; surface conditions required and competition tolerated	Sprouting ability of small trees
INTOLERANT						
Cottonwood	High	Moderate	Large	Very rapid	Wet, bare soil; no competition	Moderate
Loblolly pine	Low	Poor	Large	Rapid	Moist soil; low competition	None
Sycamore	High	Moderate	Large	Rapid	Moist, bare soil; low competition	Good
White birch	Medium	Well	Large	Rapid	Moist, bare soil; low competition	Moderate
Yellow poplar	High	Well	Large	Rapid	Moist, bare soil; low competition	Moderate
Sweetgum	High	Moderate	Large	Rapid	Moist, bare soil; moderate competition	Moderate
Black walnut	High	Well	Large	Moderate	Moist litter or soil; low competition	Moderate
Black cherry	Medium	Well	Large	Moderate	Moist litter or soil; moderate competition	Moderate
INTERMEDIATE						
Redcedar	Low	Well	Medium	Slow	Moist soil; moderate competition	None
White pine	Medium	Well	Large	Rapid	Moist litter or soil; moderate competition	None

Species						
Northern red oak	Medium	Moderate	Large	Moderate	Moist litter or soil; moderate competition	Good; seedlings excellent
Silver maple	High	Poor	Large	Rapid	Moist, bare soil; moderate competition	Good
Basswood	Medium	Moderate	Large	Moderate	Moist, bare soil; moderate competition	Good
Hickories	Medium	Well	Large	Slow	Moist litter or soil; heavy competition	Good
White ash	Medium	Moderate	Large	Moderate	Moist soil; moderate competition	Good
White oak	Medium	Well	Large	Moderate	Moist litter or soil; moderate competition	Good; seedlings excellent
Yellow birch	Medium	Moderate	Large	Moderate	Moist soil; moderate competition	Good
TOLERANT						
Dogwood	Medium	Well	Small	Slow	Moist litter or soil; heavy competition	Good
Sugar maple	Medium	Moderate	Large	Moderate	Moist litter or soil; heavy competition	Good
Beech	Medium	Moderate	Large	Moderate	Moist litter or soil; heavy competition	Good
White spruce	Medium	Poor	Large	Slow	Moist litter or soil; heavy competition	None
Hemlock	Medium	Poor	Large	Slow	Moist litter or soil; heavy competition	None

*Species are arranged in approximate order of increasing tolerance to shade.
†High: Deep moist soils where trees usually grow more than 75 ft. tall.
Medium: Moderately deep soils where trees usually grow 60 to 75 ft. tall.
Low: Dry, sandy, or thin soils where trees usually grow less than 60 ft. tall.

THE CONCEPT OF SUSTAINED YIELD

"Sustained yield" has been a time-honored goal of most forestry practice in both Europe and America. In Nature new growth and yield of wood, wildlife, and water continues on from year to year in something of a balance. Effective forest management utilizes these forest values without destroying the forest and without diminishing the yield. In a sense, we utilize what Nature "wastes." But sustained yield has not always worked according to theory. A forest or a region cannot continue to produce at some high initial level year after year. Moreover, it is seldom possible to produce a *constant* annual yield of anything, be it timber, wildlife, water, or intangible values, and this is especially true for relatively small woodlands. Such a goal is neither attainable nor necessarily desirable. Production from a forest environment varies periodically as does demand for those values.

Yet the idea of sustained yield in the sense of a more or less continuous, although fluctuating, production has great merit. We would like to keep our woodlands on a fairly even keel by harnessing the ecological behavior of Nature. On a small woodland this can only be done by harvesting a portion of the tree volume periodically, enough so that we can come back in five to ten years and do it again. For non-timber uses the forest conditions necessary for such yields must be maintained. For example, cutting irregular openings among the larger trees and some smaller trees equal to about 12 percent of the total area every ten years in hardwood forests would provide a fairly continuous yield of sawtimber, browse for deer, and habitat for diversified wildlife. In an average well-managed woodland, this would be a harvest of about 2,000 board feet per acre plus some low-quality smaller trees for pulpwood or firewood. Clearcutting the whole woodland would make sustained yield in the near future impossible. However, in some cases this might be the best alternative for timber production, as will be discussed in Chapter 5.

INTEGRATED AND MULTIPLE USE

Whenever we try to obtain several different values from the same woodland the complexity of management is increased (see Chapter 9). In a large forest different uses can be located in different parts of the forest. This practice is called "multiple use," but in another sense it is a group of single uses. Management can proceed with one predominant use at a given location, but if we want to emphasize several values from a small area, perhaps the same acre, the silviculture required may be quite different and more complex. In this case a more descriptive term would be "integrated use," as previously mentioned, and it is this that is most applicable to small private woodlands. In the current literature and mass communications, "multiple use" is used for both a group of single uses and integrated use.

On a small woodland we usually want integrated use. Ecologically, several of the possible uses are compatible, but some are not. It is mostly a matter of emphasis. Forest diversity is the key condition for wildlife, recreation, aesthetics, and watershed protection. These values tend to be compatible in a hardwood forest. Timber values are also available, but some sacrifice may be necessary, often depending on markets and other economic conditions.

It is feasible to develop a forest with a variety of species, tree sizes, tree ages, and forest openings. Suppose you are mainly interested in a continuous forest cover with maximum values for a variety of wildlife and with timber as a secondary use. You would want a range of tree sizes including some large ones, openings for food and the "edge" habitat required by wildlife, and a variety of tree species for both wildlife and timber. Openings are needed for both wildlife and tree reproduction. A variety of tree species are desirable for wildlife and timber, and this also makes a more stable forest environment. Note that this type of forest would have considerable aesthetic appeal and would offer good watershed protection. Such a forest can be developed by harvesting single large trees (if tolerant) or trees in small groups.

It has been mentioned, and it should be emphasized, that manipulation of forest vegetation must be done within limits of ecological principles and soil-site quality. Reversing the trend of ecological succession is difficult, expensive, and dangerous. It is more prudent and scientific to make the cultural modifications within the limits of the natural trends associated with the climate and the soil-site capabilities. For example, trying to introduce southern species into a northern climate will almost certainly lead to disaster. Plantations of species with high site requirements like black walnut and yellow-poplar on eroded old fields or dry ridge tops will be failures. Clearcutting on steep slopes with thin soils may degrade the site and allow an invasion of unwanted pioneer species. But medium tolerant species such as oaks, black cherry, ash, and yellow-poplar may be encouraged by providing sufficient light in openings. This occurs in nature. Foresters can speed this process by correct cutting and release.

PUTTING IT ALL TOGETHER

Ecology is a synthesizing science. It tells us what we can and cannot do if a healthy environment is desired. It provides the biological reality to fit the social goals. It is a tool of self-interest provided only that self-interest is truly understood as the long-run welfare and essential humanity of people. It teaches us that Nature, in the face of Man's destructive activities, cannot take care of itself. We must apply this synthesis of biological knowledge to cause changes and obtain results through the active culture of forests. We are irrational to pursue an opposite course that will lead to an environment we do not want. Yet, this is what we do all too often in the management of both forests and other resources.

Why do we do this? Sometimes because of ignorance but more often because of an economic commitment to environmental abuse. But this abuse can be neutralized by ecological insights which are already available. For woodlands the remedy is the intensive application of silviculture in the light of a holistic view of the forest ecosystem and its relations to people and the natural world. During the past million years, thinking Man has, for the most part, allowed the events of history to happen to him. In the case of woodlands, intensively applied ecological forestry would allow Man to make history and help create a better world. I hope you will think about this the next time you walk through your woodland.

3

The Economics of Small Woodlands

FOR MANY YEARS the small woodland in this country has been the despair of foresters and economists alike. Small woodlands contain much of the total timber and opportunity for other forest uses, but forest-management practices are minimal and the cash-and-returns picture for timber is bleak. Foresters have not entirely neglected the small woodlands, but most efforts have been ineffective. Economists have usually painted a grim financial picture, and foresters have only recently tried to motivate woodland owners toward other uses and satisfactions besides timber. But how can close to three-fourths of the forest and timber resources in the East be ignored? Obviously it cannot, and I would like to discuss some of the newer thinking and changes that make the future of the small woodland much brighter than in the past.

Previous chapters have emphasized that forestry practices are, or should be, dependent on your goals of ownership and management. The values expected from the woodland have changed, partly because the types of owners are different and partly because the social values of forests have been increasingly recognized. We could seldom show a financial profit from high-priced forest land from timber values alone, at least not when all the costs were included. Now we recognize that most owners hold their land for a variety of purposes. Timber may or may not be included among these objectives and may explain why many owners manage their woodlands at a financial loss yet are still smiling. It also helps explain why landowners have seemed to respond so slowly to the urgings of foresters to "manage" their woodlands.

THE MEANING OF WOODLAND ECONOMICS

It is necessary to discuss briefly the subject of economics and how this social science can be extended to your woodland. The word *economics*, as derived from the Greek, means "household management." Economics is normally concerned with the production, distribution, and consumption of goods involving costs and returns, usually measured by monetary units. The concept often carries a strong meaning of saving and thrift and of *material* values. Modern economists view economics as the study of human choice and the allocation of resources to satisfy human wants and needs. In recent years economists have tended to include all values which can be measured by money or some units substituting for money.

But there has been great difficulty in quantifying all the different kinds of human satisfactions and joys. One way of converting to money units is based on a market value or "value in exchange" philosophy. For example, how much less would your house be worth *without* the big maple tree in your side yard? How much more is your woodland worth on the market since you planted native ornamental shrubs and established nature trails? This method is dear to the hearts of some economists. Another means of evaluation is called the "value in use" method. How much money would you sacrifice to save the maple tree in your yard? Would you freely take $100 from the Highway Department or would you turn down $5,000 because you would rather have the tree? This is a personal matter and may have little relation to the market value. Certainly the "value in use" method is far more realistic in measuring value to *you*.

Yet, there are values in life and in nature where even this system of judgment seems crass. You might say that the satisfactions from your woodland are truly priceless, that money is not an appropriate or even a permissible medium of measurement. Sources of aesthetic and spiritual values in the forest may be priceless if you have access to no others. So it is very difficult to put financial values on your woodland which will be acceptable. Your personal value judgments, or those of any given group of people, may defy quantitative analysis and measurement.

With this background, how are the products of your woodland evaluated? Timber is largely material with a dollar value for stumpage or the cut product. Water has both material and intangible values. It has money value for both quantity and quality, although perhaps not to the owner of the watershed. Water quality in your own stream may have money value if used for recreation or fishing, and it has aesthetic value for you and your neighbors. Watershed protection has a long-term and profound material and aesthetic value for future generations — even their very existence. Wildlife has recreational value for hunting and for observation and has material value if used as meat. But no one justifies sport hunting on the basis of meat obtained. Recreation can be evaluated by dollars to you if fees are charged for services, but the people who pay the fees take their value in satisfaction. It is a little silly to measure these joys in terms of fees paid, miles traveled, or gasoline bought.

Many consider aesthetic values to be purely priceless in terms of money. But to some people there is a "trade-off" value between aesthetics and other uses. Trade-off values, however, might have little meaning unless survival or physical privation were the alternative. Only you can judge the value of woodland aesthetics to you, personally. Beauty may well have more value to you than all the timber and other values combined. Fortunately, as pointed out in Chapter 9, different woodland values are not mutually exclusive.

Two things should now be clear: (1) The economics and management of your woodland must be related to your objectives (desires), and (2) it is better to think in terms of woodland values than woodland economics, as the term has been commonly used. Values can include both quantity and quality in the sense of usefulness, desirability, importance, enjoyment, aesthetics, and even profit. Remember that many modern economists understand this and are struggling to place all types of woodland values into a generalized economic equation which considers inputs and outputs of all kinds, even those normally hidden. But perhaps some things in life should be outside a measureable unit value system. This is a profound insight believed by many but too often forgotten in everyday life. The forests of America are more than timber and more than trees. They are the cathedral of the people.

TIMBER AS A BY-PRODUCT

There is no way a small private woodland owner can justify the present high price of forested land and other fixed costs on the basis of timber values alone. Let us consider some simple facts.

Hardwood forests in the East, if *well managed* and *well stocked,* will make a net growth of 100 to 500 board feet per acre, per year, depending on the site quality. A growth of 250 board feet is probably higher than average. Stumpage values for logs vary widely depending on species, log quality, and local markets, and they change from year to year.

It is risky to use dollar values to show profit or loss from timber operations. Dollars change too rapidly. But look at it this way, fifteen or twenty years ago the value of timber growth per decade on typical forest land was roughly twice the cost of the land (for well-managed woodlands). In the mid-seventies the timber growth value per decade is usually less than half the cost of the forest land. At the same time the fixed costs — including interest, taxes, insurance, and protection — have greatly increased. These are the costs of owning land and of protecting it. They must be paid whether or not you manage the woodland.

Let us assume some reasonably current dollar values for purposes of this comparison. You can then substitute the figures for your own property at any given time. Assume you paid $200 per acre for the land, your real estate taxes are two dollars per acre annually, and let us say the costs of insurance, fencing, posting, and fire protection are only two dollars per acre each year. At 8 percent simple interest on the land investment plus the other costs, you would have a total fixed cost of $20 per acre. But you still can grow only about 200 board feet per acre annually, and this would require a very high average timber stumpage return even to equal the $20 fixed costs. Compound interest on cost of the land would make the picture considerably worse. Remember, these costs include nothing for management and technical skills or outlays for silvicultural treatments on the woodland. Make your own computations at actual current dollar values and see how timber fares when considered as the *only* return. Forest land owned by industry is an entirely different matter, and the financial accounting is far beyond the scope of this book and knowledge of the author.

However, there are ways people have made money buying land for timber alone. The best and most common way has been to buy heavily timbered tracts for a cheap price. Buying timber land with 5,000 board feet or more per acre at $5 to $10 per acre was formerly common, but this is no longer true. Another way is to buy land with immature timber at the market price and to gamble that inflation, plus timber growth plus increased land and timber prices will outrun interest, taxes, and other fixed costs. Land with good young timber is worth considerably more than bare land or land with decadent, low-quality trees.

Another good timber deal is to buy a tract which will allow rather heavy commercial thinning, improvement cutting, partial harvest cut, or a combination of these; and still leave a good stand of growing stock trees. An actual stand of hardwoods on the Kaskaskia Experimental Forest (U.S. Forest Service) in southern Illinois with 4,900 board feet per acre of sawtimber-sized trees yielded 3,700 board feet per acre in a combined improvement and partial harvest cut. This left 1,200 board feet of sawlog trees plus about 100 good trees per acre 5 to 10 inches in diameter. Nineteen years later the stand contained 7,900 board feet per acre, an average growth of 350 board feet per acre annually. The stumpage (in 1948) was worth about $20 per thousand, or $74 per acre for the 3,700 board feet cut. So in this case the investor could have paid as high as $74 per acre (minus management costs and risk factor), sold the timber stumpage which should be cut, and owned the well-stocked woodland free and clear for future growth. But, on a strictly financial basis this timber return should be compared with alternative returns from investments other than timberland.

So if timber values alone will seldom pay off to a small woodland owner at the present time, how does he justify owning the land, to say nothing of spending money for forest practices? The answer is that most private ownerships are justified on the basis of the *other forest values* we have discussed, plus speculation on rising land prices. The fixed costs can be and are charged to these non-timber values. Thus, only the direct costs such as tree planting for cash crops, stand improvement, and management costs need be charged to the timber values. Timber is treated as a by-product, and this can make the timber picture look very bright, *if* timber production does not unduly damage other values. This is where the art of silviculture is required, and this point is discussed throughout the book, especially in Chapters 9 and 10.

Suppose for example, that all the fixed costs of a woodland are charged to the non-timber values. The following actual case initiated about twenty years ago on the Kaskaskia Experimental Forest illustrates the possibilities. A 21-acre woodland in poor condition contained 64,000 board feet of sawtimber plus many cull trees of pole size and larger. There were also 756 good trees

A portion of the twenty-one-acre woodland described and evaluated in this chapter before any treatments were made. The mature and low-quality merchantable trees were cut, the cull trees killed, and the good growers of all sizes left to grow. On the whole this woodland was poorer than average.

of pole size not included in sawtimber. In two combined improvement and partial harvest cuts 37,000 board feet of merchantable logs were removed, and 1,400 cull trees were killed at a cost (at that time) of $210. The stumpage value of cut logs was then about $800. Cull trees were killed to provide more growing space for the good trees left and to help create cleared openings for new regeneration. It required about one day for a young professional forester to mark with a paint gun the merchantable trees to cut and cull trees to kill. At that time $30 per day was a fair fee for a young field forester. So the direct costs of killing cull trees and tree marking was $210 plus $30 equals $240 for the 21-acre woodland. At 6 percent simple interest this was a future cost of $14.40 per year based on direct management costs. But fifteen years after the cutting and improvement treatment the woodland had a total of 67,000 board feet of sawlogs, plus 1,239 good pole-sized trees, and had sapling reproduction in all the cut openings. Thus, the volume increased by 40,000 board feet or 2,700 board feet per year. At $30 per thousand current stumpage this was $80 per year stumpage, much higher than the $14 needed for the 6 percent simple interest on *direct costs*. In fact this is 33 percent annual simple interest earned by timber growth based on the cash outlay for timber measures alone. And the forest had a higher sawtimber volume, a larger number of good pole-size trees, a better average tree quality, and better reproduction than the original forest.

The physical data and results just described are summarized in Table 3.1. The cull trees in Table 3.1 were 5 inches and larger in diameter. Many sapling trees smaller than 5 inches grew into the pole-sized class before the second treatment and during the entire fifteen years. This accounts for the increase in pole-sized trees over the fifteen-year period. Also, some of the sawtimber volume at the end was contributed by pole-sized trees growing into the eleven-inch and larger sizes.

There are two other considerations that should be discussed with reference to Table 3.1. Suppose that *all* of the merchantable sawtimber had been cut. This would have paid an additional $540 (for the 27,000 board feet cut) or $32.40 at 6 percent interest per year as compared to the $80 received from growth on these trees. In addition, there was the growth on the good pole-sized trees which were not merchantable and not cut. Then, of course, this type of commercial clearcutting would put the owner out of the timber business for a long time and destroy the forest habitat. The second point is the uncertainty regarding the net effect of killing culls. We know this treatment increases growing space for both good growing stock trees and reproduction. We also know that after several cuts and many years such poor trees would virtually take over the forest. But we do not know the net effect in every case of cull removal on growth during the first fifteen to twenty years. Certainly much growth would have occurred even if cull trees had been left. The quality of trees in the forest must be considered over the long term.

The rate of return for timber would increase as fixed costs decreased. If timber is considered a by-product, fixed costs are zero and the rate of timber return is maximized. As the fixed costs charged to timber increases, the returns from timber can be zero or negative.

THE ECONOMICS OF INTEGRATED USE

Many foresters believe that proper silvicultural practices can enhance the production of both timber and non-timber forest values, yet there is great difficulty in measuring the economic values of the integrated use situation. Costs of forest practices are calculated in money or some physical units such as man-hours. Returns may be in terms of pleasure, enjoyment, or satisfaction. Unless you are willing and able to use the "value in exchange" or the "value in use" methods already discussed, these values do not have dollar signs. We have already noted that it is not always wise or desirable to place enjoyment in measurable quantitative units. But it is clear that non-timber values are often paramount and that a *combination of several values* may well make woodland ownership a very desirable situation indeed.

The principle can best be illustrated by the examples and estimated data already discussed in this chapter. Table 3.2 summarizes a possible situation where the returns from timber, recreation, and hunting are considerably on the optimistic side.

It is clear that increases in land values and possible government subsidies are the keys to financial profit. Government subsidies include both RECP (Rural Environmental Conservation Program) payments and free consulting services from your state service forester (see Appendix A for a listing of state forestry offices and subsidies). If these financial values materialize, or if the optimistic returns from timber, recreation, and hunting can be realized, then the costs of satisfactions are considerably reduced or eliminated. It is fortunate that most owners desire to work for integrated uses and receive multiple benefits. It helps financially and it provides satisfactions and spiritual values almost beyond price.

Table 3.1

SUMMARY OF RESULTS ON 21-ACRE POOR WOODLAND		
Original woodland	Removed in two cutting and improvement treatments	Woodland 15 years after first treatment
64,000 bd. ft. sawtimber-sized trees	37,000 bd. ft. logs	67,000 bd. ft. sawtimber-sized trees
756 good growing class pole-sized trees	None	1,239 good growing class pole-sized trees
672 cull trees	1,400 cull trees	273 cull trees

Table 3.2

TIMBER COSTS AND RETURNS	
Annual Costs per Acre	Annual Returns per Acre
Interest on land purchased at $200 . . . . . . $16 Taxes . . . . 2 Protection . . . . 2 All management and forest practices . . . . 3 TOTAL $23	Material values Timber . . . . $12 Recreation fees . . . . . . 1 Hunting fees . . . . 1 Water . . . . seldom salable Land value . . . . 0 to indefinite increase Subsidies Government subsidy . . . . . . 0 to about 15 (paid once) Satisfactions Water quality. . . . 0 to infinity Recreation . . . . . 0 to infinity Wildlife . . . . 0 to infinity Aesthetics . . . . . 0 to infinity

4

Social Values of Forest Environments

FOREST ENVIRONMENT, used in the broadest sense, affects how people live and interact with each other. To primitive man forests often provided shelter, food, and protection. In modern times we are conscious of benefits ranging from the global cycling of carbon dioxide, through timber for our homes, to the spiritual benefits ever more important in the material crush of modern living. Perhaps we are just now learning again what Wordsworth wrote nearly two hundred years ago:

> One impulse from a vernal wood
> May teach you more of man,
> Of moral evil and of good,
> Than all the sages can.

The human and social benefits from forests have been mentioned and implied many times throughout this book. This chapter will summarize and highlight the many social values of forest environments to you and to the human community. We need to heighten our understanding of the total role of the forest and to rid ourselves of the financial-materialistic tunnel vision so dominant in the past. At least we need to explore the field so that people can judge and choose for themselves.

FORESTS AND HUMAN BEHAVIOR

I am not a psychologist, and certainly all psychologists would not agree with all of what I am going to say. Yet, I write this with considerable confidence because it is how I feel, and I have observed that my feelings are common to many other men. So let me express some thoughts on this subject that may strike a responsive chord.

Forests add something to life that many of us take for granted, and others do not have the opportunity to notice one way or another. Forests are a sort of insulation against persistent and continuous contact among people. Trees and forests can soften the sharp edges of human society, moderate conflicts and irritations, and lessen the mood of harshness so common when people are crowded. A forest is a place to which to escape, a place for renewal, a place to find mental and physical contentment, a place to love. This feeling has been widespread in song, story, and poetry throughout human culture. It is ironic that some people have uselessly destroyed the beauty of the forest environment while others have found in it the very meaning of life. No one has expressed it better than Wordsworth:

> And I have felt
> A presence that disturbs me with joy
> Of elevated thoughts; a sense sublime
> Of something far more deeply interfused,
> Whose dwelling is the light of setting suns,
> And the round ocean and the living air,
> And the blue sky, and in the mind of man;
> A motion and a spirit, that impels
> All thinking things, all objects of all thought,
> And rolls through all things. Therefore am I still
> A lover of the meadows and the woods,
> And mountains; and of all that we behold
> From this green earth; of all the mighty world.

Notice that this poem uses the word *spirit*. Spiritual aspects are concerned with the life principles in man — the thinking, religious, motivating, feeling parts of man. It is perfectly valid to think of forests and forestry in spiritual terms!

In 1970 a large sugar maple tree on Long Island was bulldozed out to make way for a new shopping center. Underneath was found a small sealed metal container. Inside was a piece of parchment with this message: "This tree dedicated to beauty; planted Arbor Day 1906." At least it was beautiful for sixty-four years. This is one of the small and seemingly unavoidable tragedies that illustrates a flaw in our values and priorities. Maybe we should think about this.

DIRECT SOCIAL BENEFITS OF FORESTS

Social benefits of forests are somewhat different for rural, urban, and suburban dwellers, although some benefits are common everywhere. The intensity of environmental problems in densely populated areas is greater than in more rural areas, and the solutions and methods of solution may be quite different for each area. We will consider rural and suburban forest benefits separately, but first let us take a quick look at the whole world picture.

About one-third of the world's land area is covered with living forests. This has a profound effect on the cycling of carbon dioxide and the terrestrial heat budget of the Earth. About half of the world's photosynthesis occurs in the forests (this estimate is controversial). As every schoolchild knows, this process helps maintain the balance between oxygen and carbon dioxide in the atmosphere. Forest destruction since the Stone Age has released several times more total carbon dioxide than all the burning of fossil fuels in modern times. A fair estimate is that 10 percent of the radiant energy reaching the earth is used in transpiration of water from green leaves. This has an unknown but large effect on world climate. The world, of course, would be unlivable without green plants. Without forests, slow but profound changes would occur in the climate and atmosphere, and the soil mantle on mountain slopes would quickly wash away. Forests are an absolutely vital part of the Earth's ecosystem, of which we are a part.

What about social benefits of a more local nature? The eastern United States is probably the greatest meeting place of people and forests in the world. The region is two-thirds forested but, at the same time, heavily populated. Topography is the key factor. People are concentrated in cities, mostly near the coast, but large forested open spaces exist on the rolling and often steep and rocky terrain. To village and rural dwellers financial returns from timber and recreation from the forests are significant. But this is not to say that non-city people do not enjoy the amenities and the aesthetic values of the woodlands. That is why many of you live there, and this trend is increasing. Both the people who live near the forests and the people who *travel* to the forests seek enjoyment and spiritual values. This includes clean air, quiet, and a chance to study and contemplate Nature, as well as the usual outdoor recreation activities discussed in Chapter 7. All this presents something of a problem to the landowner. In the European tradition, many people feel they have a right of free access to open space. In a sense they do, perhaps not entirely free but at least reasonable access. No government can long survive unless it can make some provision for its citizens to enjoy forests and other open space, and government must work with owners of open space to assure fairness to all.

Urban and suburban trees and forests can provide all the above social benefits except timber, and more. Trees and forests change the microclimate of suburban and urban areas and alter the visual impact of the landscape. These are the key elements which can revolutionize a heavily populated environment. Trees provide shade, decrease long-wave radiation, and cool the air. They reduce wind and intercept rain and snow. Groups or belts of trees can deaden noise and screen eye- and ear-polluting sources such as airports, factories, shopping centers, junk yards, and other points of ugliness. Trees in congested areas can stimulate some sense of Nature, or at least promote a good feeling about where we have to live. As creative objects in formal landscape design, trees and shrubs have been used almost universally throughout the world. The state of this art is very high, yet relatively little has been done in heavily congested areas, especially if the people living there are poor. The social benefits of trees and forests in heavily populated areas have hardly been realized; the effort has hardly been made!

What are the chances of continued realization of the social values from urban forests which we have discussed? Probably not very great if present trends continue. The population of the United States has doubled in the last fifty-two years, but the rate of processing materials, a measure of consumption, doubled in the last fourteen years. Thus, we are consuming more *per person*, and much of this is nonessential or luxury consumption. This trend cannot continue. The use of all pesticides, by the way, has been doubling every seven years. If these trends continue at the same rate, soon there will be no place for forests, or they will be so polluted and abused they will gradually disappear. Thus, the social values of forests cannot be separated from population, consumption, life style, and the total environment. If we do not solve these

A diversified woodland surrounding a lake. This parkland area is accessible to urban populations and, if correctly managed, can contribute greatly to the social welfare of the region. (Photo by Albert Meyer, Southern Illinois University)

problems Man will, in a treeless world, become diminished in spirit and fulfillment.

It should never be forgotten that wood products from timber also have a vital social value. We often think of timber as a materialistic value, and so it is, but the world would be greatly diminished in both wealth and beauty without wood. Wood is a renewable and non-polluting material indispensible for modern gracious living. It has a highly tangible social worth which can be produced concurrently with the environmental values of forests.

5

Timber Production

REES GROW in response to physiological and ecological factors, and except for acute and sustained destruction, they grow despite mistreatment or use by man. The forester does not grow trees; he merely regulates to some degree the character of a forest community and its components for a particular use. A dash of humility is an essential part of the forester's wisdom.

In growing timber products (almost always integrated with other uses) two classes of cutting treatments are usually made. One is made during the development of the trees and stand and is called "intermediate cutting." The second is made when some trees are mature and when new reproduction is desired. These are called harvest or "regeneration cuts." It is important that these distinctions be understood.

Intermediate treatments or cuts are made for the following purposes: (1) to free desirable seedlings and saplings from competition, (2) to thin the trees to desirable numbers, (3) to cull out the poorer and the worthless trees, and (4) to prune lower branches from the bole (tree stem) so as to prevent knots in the lumber. The first three of the above treatments may also yield salable products.

Regeneration cuts are made to harvest trees at some determined maturity and to provide space for new reproduction. In a forest or woodland both types of cutting may or may not occur on the same acre at the same time. On bare land, or where desirable natural regeneration does not occur, artificial planting or seeding may be done to regenerate the forest.

TREE CLASSES

The idea of tree classes is most helpful in both intermediate and regeneration cutting. Trees are classified on the basis of their vigor and usefulness for timber products. Tree classes tell the owner or forest manager the present and future value of a tree and whether it should be left to grow, harvested, or perhaps killed by girdling or herbicides. It must be emphasized, however, that actions would vary for different objectives and methods of regeneration. This practice will be illustrated later in this chapter.

The suggested tree classes for *timber uses* and a brief description of each are listed below. You may need the help of a forester to identify them.

1. *Good growers:* Trees that should be left to grow; trees of desirable species having the vigor, form, quality, and position in the stand to insure future quality growth.

2. *Mature crop trees:* Merchantable trees, generally sound and healthy, that have reached the economic cutting sizes. Maturity is usually based on some percentage rate of value return. If the value return falls below some acceptable level the tree is a candidate for harvest (but this may not be the only consideration). Good timber trees should not be cut for sawlogs or veneer until they are 18 to 24 inches in diameter, depending on quality and growth rate.

3. *Sound, low-quality trees:* Merchantable trees that are sound but with poor form, short boles, or excessive knots and other defects. They will live a long time but are earning a low rate of return as compared to good growers. They should be harvested but will not be lost if the cutting is postponed. They may, however, interfere with the growth of better trees.

4. *High-risk trees:* Merchantable trees which have a low or negative rate of return and which, because of age, size, rot, low vigor, or other condition, may die or lose value before the next harvest. Such trees should be cut as soon as possible.

5. *Cull trees:* Trees not merchantable now for anything except firewood and which are not expected to become merchantable in the future. These trees occupy growing space and should be eliminated by killing or felling.

For wildlife and aesthetics some cull trees as well as trees in other classes would be useful. These aspects will be discussed in Chapters 6, 7, and 9.

This tree is a good grower as described in the text under "Tree Classes." It is making a good economic return as well as contributing to non-timber values of the woodland; it should be left to grow.

A mature oak tree. The financial return has fallen below an acceptable rate of interest and the tree should be cut along with others in a small group unless other values dictate that it be left.

A sound, low-quality tree that will
continue to live for a long time but is
earning a low rate of return for
timber. It should be cut to favor
good growers.

A high risk and over-mature tree that may die or lose value before the next harvest. It should be harvested unless it is especially valuable for wildlife.

This sugar maple is a cull tree and worthless for future growth. It has been injured, rot has entered through large branch stubs, and the tree should be killed or used for firewood.

The basal scar on this ash was caused by past fire damage, and the crooks were caused by severe damage while the tree was a sapling. The tree is a cull and should be killed or used for firewood.

APPLICATION OF TREE CLASSES

A common type of woodland is composed of trees of several to many species, ages, sizes, and conditions. Often the forest has been heavily cut in the past with the best trees taken out. The poorer trees and culls have been left. Repeated fires have caused butt scars on some trees. But normally, new saplings and poles are filling in the openings or growing in the understory. Such forests often need one or more of the following operations: (1) release of young growth from overstory competition of trees not wanted as growing stock, (2) harvest of low-quality and high-risk trees to reduce competition to good growers, (3) elimination of cull trees for the same reason, and (4) harvest of mature trees for economic reasons and to provide space for new regeneration. Any openings created for regeneration should be about one-eighth acre or larger in size (may be smaller in northern hardwoods). Openings might be created by cutting a combination of any or all tree classes except good growers. In some cases good growers are so few in number that the best economic practice is to clearcut and start with new seedlings (but this would have serious disadvantages for integrated objectives if large parts of the woodland were clearcut).

In intermediate cutting, the chief products are pulpwood and firewood from the trees not suitable for future quality logs. This kind of market is a distinct advantage to the owner. The aim is to improve the average tree quality of the forest and to reduce the density to favor the better trees. Good growers or mature trees would not be cut except in over-dense groups. Creation of openings should be avoided, though gaps of ten to fifteen feet between crowns are not excessive. In general, a continuous crown cover would be maintained. In regeneration cutting, on the other hand, the products are usually sawlogs or veneer bolts, and the aim is to create clean open spaces large enough for the successful reproduction of the desired species. In most cases only the good growers would be left, ideally in groups with crowns no farther apart than ten to fifteen feet. Other forms of regeneration cutting include clearcutting, clearcutting in strips or other patterns, and clearcutting with various numbers of trees left for seed and shelter for the new seedlings. Any method used should be in harmony with silvical characteristics of the species and with your management objectives. Indeed, it should be emphasized that good timber silviculture is usually good silviculture for integrated uses, as explained in Chapter 9.

A typical situation in a previously unmanaged hardwood forest which had been partially cut several decades earlier. Shown here is a group of mature, over-mature, and cull trees occupying about a quarter-acre. Many of the surrounding trees are good growers and should not be cut. Harvesting these large trees will create an opening for new regeneration and better conditions for wildlife.

MAINTAINING FOREST GROWING STOCK

If you could do but one thing on your woodland it could be to maintain the good growing stock trees. The greatest error in past forestry practice in America has been the liquidation of immature good growers in combination with leaving the cull and low-quality trees. It takes thirty to sixty years for the average hardwood tree to reach small sawlog size. While salable, such trees have a low value and unit value. In growing from sixteen to twenty-two inches in diameter during the next thirty to sixty year period a tree will nearly triple in sawlog volume and easily increase five times in value. You should aim toward maintaining a proportion of trees in this high increase range. Cutting immature trees is poor economics and usually poor integrated use.

Thus, the first stage of a tree's life involves establishment or building the photosynthetic plant for producing high-value lumber or veneer. The only timber value at this point is for pulpwood, and pulpwood stumpage value is low compared to quality logs. Then, after thirty to sixty years has been invested, the tree begins to increase rapidly in value up to some point called "economic maturity." Actually the tree may continue to increase in value far beyond this point, but in relation to other trees in the forest, and to an acceptable rate of interest return, the tree is deemed mature and cut. For most species in the East this point is reached between about 18 and 24 inches in diameter, depending on the growth rate and the product to be harvested.

So when you cut good-quality immature trees you are throwing away most of the thirty to sixty years already invested in them. Luckily Nature has already made the investment usually without benefit of Man's wisdom. We can at least accept the gift gratefully.

NATURAL REGENERATION

When trees are cut or eliminated, and when surrounding trees cannot fill in the gaps, new seedlings or sprouts must develop if the forest is to be perpetuated, regardless of the objectives of management. Nature does this by natural regeneration from seed produced from nearby trees or by regeneration from sprouts. Man can modify this process by preparing the seed bed, by regulating the amount of light received, and by reducing the competition from

A young hardwood stand marked for a combined thinning and improvement cutting that will provide more space for the remaining trees to grow and allow more growth of wildlife food plants on the forest floor.

In this case the young saplings should be released from the competition of the large, mainly worthless, overstory trees marked with an X, thus allowing full growth of the saplings. In some cases large cull trees may be left for wildlife food and shelter or even for visual appeal.

This is the correct way to girdle (kill) a cull tree when such action proves necessary. Most trees will die within a year, and possible pollution from herbicides is thus avoided.

Pruning high-quality crop trees improves the woodland and will provide relaxation and exercise for the owner. The worker is using a sectional aluminum pruning saw.

A portion of a mixed-oak woodland seven years after an improvement cutting. The trees left were correctly spaced good growers.

The large cull beech was girdled about ten years earlier, and space created has been filled in by saplings of yellow-poplar responding to the greatly increased light and soil moisture.

unwanted plants. The one overall and essential requirement for regeneration and seedling development is *space*. Some species can start growth and persist for many years under the shade of a forest canopy, but some adequate area of horizontal and vertical space is required for growth into the main forest canopy.

The factors and ecological relationships influencing natural reproduction are exceedingly complex (see Chapter 2). The requirements for different species are generally known, but significant control of species composition can only be carried out by an experienced professional. Fortunately, however, Nature usually provides some kind of tree reproduction which is well adapted to the climate and site. In a hardwood or mixed forest, seed of one or more species is usually abundant every year because of the many species. Some species are light-seeded, some are heavy-seeded; some seed matures in the spring and some in the fall; and seed dispersal may occur from early spring throughout the winter. In addition to seed, the usually abundant sprouting after fire or cutting and the persistence of oak root stocks in the soil provide abundant reproduction. Hardwood litter decomposes rapidly, providing a good seedbed and maintaining fertility in the topsoil. The seedlings of many hardwood species can survive under shade for relatively long periods and respond quickly when opened to overhead light. Oak seedling sprouts persist in the understory for many years. Intolerant species (see Chapter 2) require sunlight soon after germination, and thus develop only in forest openings or cleared areas. The amount of reproduction is usually abundant but the *kind* is less certain. When mixed species occur the desired ones can be favored by a weeding treatment which eliminates competitors. Fortunately, the better timber species tend also to be the fastest growing and often emerge unaided.

CHOOSING A METHOD OF REGENERATION CUTTING

With the preceding information as background, and with timber objectives in mind, how do you choose the best system of cutting to harvest the trees and assure regeneration? Here you need the advice of a forester, but as the owner, you should know some of the principles and possibilities for action.

The standard methods generally from the lightest to the heaviest cutting are: (1) single tree selection, (2) group selection, (3) shelter wood, (4) seed tree, and (5) clearcutting. Below are listed some of the conditions under which each of these regeneration cutting methods might well be used, along with a brief description of the method.

Single Tree Selection

A system where single mature trees are cut with the expectation that regeneration from seed and seedling sprouts will develop in the small openings created is called single tree selection. This practice leads to an uneven-aged forest.
1. Northern hardwood and northern coniferous forests.
2. An uneven-aged forest of mixed species and a wide range of diameters and tree classes.
3. An adequate number of large mature trees, plus trees in other tree classes, to make an operable harvest cut.

Group Selection

A system where groups of trees are cut with the expectation that regeneration from seed and seedling sprouts will develop in the openings from about one-eighth to one-half acre in size is called group selection. This practice leads to an uneven-aged forest. (Group selection may merge into patch cutting and thence into clearcutting). The essential point is that sufficient sunlight must be received for regeneration of less tolerant species (see Chapter 2).
1. Especially Appalachian hardwood, oak-hickory, and oak-pine forests. It may also be used in northern hardwood and northern coniferous forests.
2. An uneven-aged forest of mixed species and a wide range of diameters and tree classes where trees of the same age or size tend to occur in small irregular groups, like a mosaic.
3. The trees in some of the groups are mature or merchantable high-risk and low-quality trees, and the size of the resultant openings would be large enough for successful regeneration.
4. The forest contains groups of good growing trees of pole and small sawtimber sizes interspersed with areas needing regeneration.

These selection methods are most applicable for integrated values.

Shelterwood

A system where a partial cover of the best trees is left to provide seed and partial shade (shelter) for obtaining and developing the regeneration is called shelterwood. After seedlings have become established, the overstory trees are cut. This practice leads to an even-aged forest.

1. Especially useful for areas of pure white pine in the northern hardwood forests. It may also be used in the southeastern coniferous forest for pines.
2. Even-aged forests of mature trees where regeneration of the species benefits from partial shade and a plentiful source of seed.

Seed Tree

A clearcutting system where all trees are harvested except five to ten trees per acre to provide seed is called seed tree. This leads to an even-aged forest.

1. Loblolly and shortleaf pine in the southeastern coniferous forest.
2. Even-aged forests of mature trees of intolerant species.

Clearcutting

Clearcutting removes all trees on an area down through the sapling sizes. This practice leads to an even-aged forest. Clearcutting often removes only the merchantable trees, leaving the small and cull trees. Regeneration is obtained from seedlings already present, seed present in the litter, and sprouts from cut stumps. No seed trees are left. At the present time clearcutting practices in this country are being abused, even when timber is the dominant use.

1. Has been used in all forest types but is best adapted to pioneer species such as jack pine, aspen, and cottonwood; and to southeastern coniferous and oak-pine forests.
2. Even-aged forests of mature trees of intolerant species.
3. Even-aged stands of any species composed of mature, high-risk, low-quality, and cull trees that have insufficient growing stock to form an "acceptable" stand (see References).
4. Uneven-aged or irregular forests where the overstory is

A typical oak-hickory forest in the Midwest before any management and about forty to fifty years after a rather heavy partial cut. The stand contains many cull and low-quality trees as well as good growers. Most of the trees are immature, though a cut is needed to harvest the low-quality and high-risk trees and to eliminate the cull trees. Some openings could be made for new regeneration. This forest was subsequently commercially clearcut (see next two photographs).

composed of mature, high-risk, low-quality and cull trees and where growing stock will not form an "acceptable" stand. This could be an area of 2 or 3 acres or a whole ownership.

It must be emphasized that other objectives might change or modify the method of regeneration cutting. Owners might sacrifice some timber values to increase wildlife, recreation, or aesthetic values, but in most cases timber values fit in nicely with other values. These subjects are discussed in Chapters 6, 7, and 9.

YIELD OF TIMBER

The yield of timber varies greatly from place to place and depends on site quality, stocking and structure of the forest stand, age or age distribution of the stand, past history, and forest type. In this country the volume of yield is usually placed on an annual and per acre basis and expressed in board feet, cubic feet, or cords. Sawlogs or veneer logs are measured in board feet. There are several different log scales; International is the most accurate and Doyle greatly underestimates the actual board foot scale. Pulpwood is measured in several different sizes of "cords." The standard cord is 128 cubic feet of stacked wood. Green weight is increasingly being used to measure pulpwood. Cubic feet are sometimes used to measure the wood volume and growth of an entire stand of trees, but this is a technical procedure. Round tapered trees must be converted into square cubic feet. The woodland owner should have professional advice before selling his valuable timber.

The current net growth of individual woodlands may vary from zero to 1,000 or more board feet per acre annually. The total growth in standard cords may be from zero to five or more per acre annually. A sawtimber hardwood forest which averages 200 board feet in growth per acre per year is doing quite well. But forests on rich bottomlands or on upland cove sites often grow in excess of 500 board feet. However, statewide growth averages as determined by various forest surveys in the East are more likely to lie in the range of 50 to 100 board feet or one-half to one cord per acre annually.

How much is your woodland growing? Only repeated measurements, correctly done over five to ten year periods can tell you. But Table 5.1 lists some rough sideboards that will at least provide

The same commercially clearcut forest five years after cutting. All the merchantable sawtimber trees were cut. There was no market for pulpwood, and no cull trees were killed.

The same commercially clearcut forest twelve years after cutting. New regeneration has started, but the growing space is largely occupied by cull and low-quality trees.

some guidance. The amounts are *net* board feet per acre annually measured by the International Scale. It is also assumed that the woodland trees range into the sawtimber sizes. Small trees have no board feet volume because they are not usable until they are at least 11 inches in diameter; then they grow into measured volume all at once.

For pine pulpwood production, a yield of two standard cords per acre annually is reasonably good. The stand is generally harvested at about age thirty to thirty-five years. For hardwood pulp production, trees are harvested at age forty to forty-five years, and a yield of one to two cords per year is reasonable. In most woodlands, however, pulpwood should be taken in thinnings or improvement cuts to favor high-quality sawtimber trees. Such a cut would normally yield five to ten cords per acre.

REGULATION OF WOODLANDS

Regulation of your woodland by timber cutting is a means of attaining the "sustained yield" discussed in Chapter 2. It also insures that your woodland will continue to *exist* as you want it for non-timber values and continue to yield timber products from time to time. This does not mean that you can or should harvest a fixed amount annually or at some rigid interval of time. It means that harvest cuts can be flexible for both amount and interval between cuts but designed to maintain a continuous well-stocked forest with a reasonably well-balanced distribution of tree size and age classes. (See the booklet listed in the Appendix published by the Illinois Technical Forestry Association or obtain professional advice.)

The general goal, if you have a well-stocked woodland, is to harvest approximately the growth for the growing cycle: the time between harvest cuts. Thus, the woodland retains about the same volume. But growth occurs on all the trees. Cutting should be concentrated on the larger or mature trees, but it should also include some smaller trees of poorer quality. Between cuts, smaller trees of about 16 to 20 inches in diameter grow into harvest trees of 18 to 22 inches in diameter. If the woodland has a good balance of tree sizes, the trees of each lower diameter class will grow into larger sizes, and periodic cuts of harvest trees, as well as thinning among smaller sizes, are possible and desirable. In a typical case this would mean harvesting small openings (group selection) equal to 10 to 15 percent of the area and 20 to 30 percent of the log volume every eight to twelve years. On an average hardwood site this would be a harvest of 1,500 to 2,000 board feet of logs per acre; on excellent sites it would be considerably higher.

But forest stands or woodlands are seldom balanced in this way. Because of past practices and abuse there may be far too many large trees or too many small trees in relation to other sizes; and there may be many low-quality and over-mature trees. This is why cutting cycle and amount cut must be flexible. A wise owner will gradually manipulate his woodland to attain his objectives — often integrated uses including wildlife, aesthetics, and recreation along with timber. This would usually involve a rough balancing of diverse tree sizes as discussed above and openings for new regeneration. It is imperative that cutting treatments be adjusted as you go along. There should be no rigid, permanent plans. Adjustments toward the goal must be guided by a formal or informal continuous forest inventory at about ten year intervals to determine the nature of your woodland — the number, species, size, and condition of the trees.

The key, then, to regulating your woodland is a flexible approach based on and modified by: (1) forest growth, (2) tree size distribution, (3) stand condition (tree classes), (4) condition of wood commodity markets, (5) personal preference and need for money, and (6) satisfactions other than timber objectives. You will not usually have an exactly even flow of timber products, but you will be practicing sustained yield in the truest sense of the term.

PLANTING TREES FOR TIMBER PRODUCTION

The public generally has some glaring misconceptions about tree planting in America. Tree planting is a difficult, complex, and exacting practice. Over the years there has been a higher percentage of failures than for any other forestry practice, especially on small private ownerships. Popular and persistent myths about planting are still rampant: You can plant trees anywhere they will grow. Any old method of planting will do. Plant whatever species suits your fancy. No site preparation is required. No care after planting is needed. Use seedlings from any available source.

All the above statements are false! Except for southern pines, plantings on private, non-industrial lands in the East have, for timber purposes, been largely failures.

What can you do to obtain successful plantations on abandoned old fields and on clearcut or burned areas which have not regenerated naturally? First, you need the professional advice of an experienced forester. Here are the points the forester must take into account:

1. The planting area should be subject to protection from destructive factors and sudden changes of land use.

2. The species selected should be adapted to the climate, and the seed source (parent trees) should be native to the general region of the planting site.

3. The species must be adapted to the *existing* soil-site conditions, not what they were when the former forest was present. Pine species are much easier to plant successfully than hardwoods.

4. It is best to plant mixtures of several species in a group arrangement. A diversified plantation offers greater resistance to insects and diseases, providing better wildlife habitat and a greater variety of timber products.

5. Site treatments and planting methods must be designed to obtain good survival of planted seedlings.

6. Nursery seedlings must be healthy, moist, and fresh.

7. Needed care of the plantation after planting must be provided, usually release from choking vegetation and thinning when the trees are older. If you are not willing or able to touch all of these bases, it would be better to save the money and let Nature do it the slow way.

Tree planting is done for many other purposes than timber production. These purposes will be discussed elsewhere, but the general principles of successful establishment are the same. Planting ornamentals presents a different situation. Large trees with earth balls are planted, the site is carefully prepared, trees have no competition, they receive intensive care, and the final objective is not necessarily a tall tree requiring a high site quality.

Table 5.1

EXPECTED GROWTH RATES IN BOARD FEET		
General site quality	Original woodland; no silviculture, poor trees and culls still present, low stocking	Silviculture practiced; treatments made and stocking of good trees built up to near optimum
Excellent: Rich, well-drained alluvial bottomlands	250	800
Good: Upland coves and lower slopes	150	500
Medium: Upper and middle slopes in uplands	100	300
Poor: Ridge tops and upper southerly slopes in uplands	50	150

6

Wildlife and Fish Habitat

ILDLIFE AND FISH are a valuable natural resource which make life more enjoyable while reminding us of our humble origins, our closeness to Nature, and the common environment essential to all life. These are spiritual values, but wildlife may also provide some economic returns to woodland owners. Forests and woodlands, together with adjacent farmlands, provide the home for many kinds of wildlife. In this forest habitat they live, eat, and breed.

It is crucial to understand that Man may either stabilize, destroy, or enhance this habitat for the use of wildlife. Experienced ecologists and foresters can manipulate and maintain an entire forest environment to satisfy the requirements of various wildlife and fish populations, but individual woodlands are best managed as part of a whole rural community — as a balance of the claims of conservation, agriculture, recreation, and housing. In encouraging a viable population of deer, for example, community cooperation is vital. In some cases this has been accomplished through wildlife cooperatives formed by several landowners. With the exception of plans for such wide-ranging species as deer, however, it is not wise to wait too long for cooperation of neighbors, because much wildlife is confined to your own woodland. Improvements will enhance the whole area, and your example and good results will be a potent persuader. But in the end, community action and cooperation among neighbors is necessary to preserve the character of the area (the reason you bought there in the first place) and to provide the best wildlife management.

We should first distinguish between wildlife and game. Wildlife includes all wild living creatures in the environment, songbirds as well as ruffed grouse, and snakes as well as deer. Broadly speaking, the word *wildlife* should also include fish, but general usage in many states has excluded fish.

The word *game* applies to those species of wildlife which are hunted and killed for sport and food, usually under legal restraints; *game fish* is used in this same sense. When we speak of "game management" we mean management to control the population and habitat of game. Wildlife management is a broader concept and implies ecological management for all natural wildlife in an area.

The legal status of wildlife and fish in this country poses a problem for the landowner. Wildlife and fish belong to the people, their harvest is controlled by the state, but the land where the wildlife lives and the shores of streams are owned and controlled by the landowner. A landowner cannot kill restricted wildlife on his own land except under the law. Yet he can forbid hunters or others from trespassing on his land or fishing from his stream banks. This division makes an effective program of wildlife management very difficult. Sportsmen buy a license from the state allowing them the privilege of taking game; yet they have no direct responsibility for maintaining wildlife or its habitat and are often destructive of property and other values dear to the landowner. Consequently, landowners increasingly are using "no trespassing" signs as a device to protect the woodland values. No one can blame them, yet in the absence of natural predators some wildlife species can only be kept within desired limits if Man acts as a predator. For example, deer in some parts of the Lake States and Adirondacks became so numerous they prevented normal tree reproduction, and many deer died of starvation. The control of game populations for a workable balance between the game and its supporting environment is a problem which must always be borne in mind, even though the solution is not always clear. Sometimes fee hunting and per-acre land leases are partial solutions. In some cases special hunts have been organized. In any event, each landowner will want to protect his environmental and wildlife values but with the knowledge that some wildlife may be or needs to be harvested.

The pressure of land use by sportsmen is rendered critical for the landowner by the rapidly expanding demand for hunting and fishing recreation. People have more free time and disposable income for recreation. Transportation to all sorts of rural and wild areas becomes easier and easier. "Opening day" throughout the country is becoming an unfunny joke. The number of hunting and fishing licenses issued each year is at least 35 million. Thus more and more people are wanting to use a decreasing amount of land. But there is one counteracting force. There is a growing number of people who love wildlife, who like to know that it is there, and who are happy to photograph and watch. Such aesthetic and spiritual values are just as real as hunting values; many landowners treasure these values, and management can provide them for both the woodland owner and the community.

WILDLIFE HABITAT MANAGEMENT

To attain success you must first decide on your objectives and be willing and able to use the intensity of management required for at least your minimum objectives. Will it be one game species, a limited number of game species, or a diversity of wildlife? In deciding this, you should always remember that the habitat will likely be favorable to several species. Management practices with heavy emphasis on only one species are difficult, for it is not easy to exclude species. Balance rather than specialization is the best ecological management. Intensive measures to maintain a monoculture of game promote a "game farm" with all its limitations and evils of instability. Maintaining a diversity of species through a diversified habitat is usually easier and more in tune with ecological principles.

A definite limitation on wildlife management is the total site quality, sometimes called carrying capacity. Among aspects of carrying capacity are terrain, available water, the overall fertility of the soil, and its ability to produce food. Wildlife does occur on impoverished and dry sites, but harsh conditions limit both the diversity of species and the total number of animals and birds. Site quality also limits the intensity of management practices (such as planting) which may be feasible. Nature alone may be the best manager on poor sites.

The single most important word for describing favorable conditions for a variety of life is *diversity*. Picture a forest environment with numerous species of trees, shrubs, and vines; several forest types on different sites; a number of tree age classes; numerous sunlit openings with their accompanying edges; and a variety of understory vegetation. Imagine further the presence of den trees and other favorable breeding and resting places, plentiful wildlife food species, and trees providing winter shelter. Consider that all these features can occur on a relatively small area (your woodland). If you can hold this picture in your mind, you have gone far in understanding the habitat diversity needed for a wide range of wildlife species.

The culture of forest stands through cutting or other means provides a way of obtaining diversity or, if desired, creating special conditions in the forest to achieve special objectives. At present and in the past, *cutting for timber products has had a greater influence on wildlife in this country than any active program of wildlife management.* For example, clearcutting may be good or bad, depending on what is wanted. Clearcutting large areas would greatly increase the deer browse for four to eight years, but squirrels, wild turkey, grouse, and many songbirds would lose some favorable and diversified habitat. Alternatively, light partial cutting would increase deer browse slightly and would favor grouse and songbirds. The great effects of timber cutting in this country have been largely unintentional. Conscious cultural practices in forests for wildlife management objectives are still infrequent and limited.

What specific effects do various cultural practices in the forest have on wildlife habitat? Reducing the tree density increases the forest floor vegetation and provides larger trees with larger tops and limbs and with a greater seed (nut and acorn) production. Creating openings of about one-eighth acre or larger provides browse and other food plants and a longer perimeter of edges for nesting, food, and shelter. Release cuttings stimulate the growth of the favored trees or plants. Improvement cuttings favor certain individual trees for wildlife such as large oaks in a pine forest or den trees in a hardwood or mixed forest. Planting may be used (with great care) to introduce food or shelter species into any forest — planting conifers for winter cover in a hardwood forest, for example. Clearcutting a small portion of a woodland having mature trees may provide extra browse and produce economic returns in timber as well.

Special measures used in active game management include providing water, creating food plots, and fertilizing soil. An occasional drinking pond will extend the range and provide better distribution of deer. Openings here and there in the forest can be cultivated, fertilized, and seeded in grains that are acceptable to wildlife. Blanket fertilization over large areas is probably not a good practice because of the danger of pollution of streams. Lime, however, is often needed, and its moderate use is generally beneficial and carries little danger of pollution.

Wild native fish require rather specific conditions for reproduction, growth, and maturity. Trout cannot survive in warm, dirty water, and they cannot reproduce unless the water habitat is just right. Forest cuttings and logging that cause the water to become warm in summer and loaded with silt and leached nutrients will simply kill the trout or prevent any future reproduction. Planted trout usually live for a few months until they get caught by some eager fisherman, but they seldom reproduce, and the "put and take" must be on an annual basis. Fingerlings, however, may be stocked in good trout waters with the expectation that they will grow to legal size. Trout streams require treatment that will preserve the special and delicately balanced stream conditions natural to trout. For example, trout require a high oxygen tension which occurs only in cool water, no warmer than 72-74°F. Bass can tolerate silt and warm water but not heavy amounts of debris or pollution. Your woodland will be best for the native fish when the watershed cover is disturbed the least — when stream banks are left shaded by trees, when logging debris is kept out of streams, and when roads are built in a manner to protect streams from mud and silt. (Specific measures for fish management are discussed in the References.)

HABITAT REQUIREMENTS
OF SOME COMMON GAME SPECIES*

A brief description of habitat requirements of several game species will serve to illustrate and clarify the silvicultural practices involved. More detailed descriptions, including other species, are available in the References in Appendix C.

Whitetail Deer

The home range of deer is not generally wide, but the daily

---

*Parts of this section have been adapted from a report by a former student at Virginia Polytechnic Institute, Andrew B. Carey.

range may sometimes extend to several miles. The winter range, at least in heavy snow country, is greatly restricted. Sometimes deer may disappear from your woodland in winter. Deer are forest inhabitants but reach greater densities where the total area of brushland food supply (forest reproduction) is large. In this country, deer population has exploded in several regions after extensive timber harvesting. However, woody vegetation grows out of the reach of deer in four to eight years; thus some cutting must be carried out continuously to provide year-round fresh browse if a large population is to be maintained. It is best if food and shelter are scattered throughout the range so as to keep the deer moving about and to help prevent restriction of the winter range.

Within the deer's range it is preferable to have a diversity of plant species, forest types, and age classes plus some nonforest land such as fields and orchards. This is common in the East. Deer will eat whatever vegetable matter is available, including browse, grass, grain, herbs, fruit, and acorns. During the northern winters they need conifers for shelter and food, especially northern white cedar. Under good habitat conditions it is safe to harvest 20-30 percent of the herd annually. If the deer are interfering with other desired forest uses a larger harvest would be justified.

The following treatment may improve the habitat for deer: (1) Harvest mature timber by clearcutting in small blocks or create cleared openings in the forest as in group selection. (2) Stimulate the growth of food plants on the forest floor by reducing the stand density as in thinning, improvement, and release cuttings; the heavier the cut the greater will be the response of understory vegetation of all kinds. (3) Maintain existing hardwood cover of different ages and convert large unbroken blocks of conifers to mixed forests. (4) Gradually convert large even-aged forests to uneven-aged forests with sustained yield characteristics. (5) Release fruit-bearing shrubs and trees and prune wild or old orchard fruit trees for winter food. (6) Plant trees for food and shelter such as northern white cedar within its range. Clumps of conifers within large unbroken tracts of hardwoods are usually helpful. (7) In northern climates develop connecting lanes of protecting conifers between adjacent deer yards to encourage movement of deer. Deer will also follow well-worn snowmobile paths, and these paths may be used by deer to find better food and shelter. (8) If feasible, protect the deer from highway slaughter and the accompanying loss of property and even human life. This is a most difficult

Deer browse hardwood and shrubby twigs and buds, especially in winter. Most timber cutting produces more woody sprouts, and, properly done, deer and timber management can be compatible.

problem and should eventually be settled by management practices such as the use of fences as an integral part of highway construction.

Ruffed Grouse

The range of grouse is restricted to about a quarter of a mile, and the various habitat requirements should be included in a rather small area. During the winter and the spring nesting season grouse use dense forest areas with mixed hardwoods and conifers. During the summer and fall they prefer more open, brushy areas. Grouse eat a great variety of vegetable matter and some animal matter. Young grouse eat insects almost exclusively. For high grouse production broods must have places to find insects, such as openings with a variety of grasses and herbs. In general, a favorable habitat is a mixture of hardwoods and conifers of all ages with numerous well-distributed openings from about 100 to 600 feet in diameter. Aspen is particularly favored by grouse. Unbroken large areas of either clearcutting or dense uncut forests are unfavorable.

Some more intensive and specific management practices for grouse are as follows: (1) reduce forest density to favor the growth of food shrubs already present; (2) make cuttings that will release and favor winter food species such as grape, birch, beech, aspen, cherry, and hophornbeam; (3) plant or release groups of conifers, especially hemlock, in the understory of hardwood forests; (4) plant or encourage fruit-bearing woody plants; (6) construct slash piles in bramble thickets along the edges of forest stands for nesting and protection.

Grouse are closely attuned to their environment and they can become eliminated quickly unless favorable habitat is maintained. An annual harvest of more than two per nesting pair is probably excessive, but habitat is more important than hunting pressure. Unlike deer and rabbits grouse seem naturally to maintain a rather sparse population, even when conditions are favorable. Grouse are wild; unlike quail they do not mix well with people and agriculture. In Man's world they need consideration, help, and even a little love.

Grouse require wooded cover for nesting. This grouse hen is well concealed on the forest floor.

Wild Turkey

Wild turkey are also creatures of the wild and do not thrive in close proximity to man and his works. A flock will range over about four square miles. Turkeys require open forests of mast-producing hardwoods, but some mixture of conifers is beneficial; cover should be varied in type and age, and the area may well contain scattered openings and some cultivated land. Turkeys eat acorns, other seeds and nuts, fleshy fruits, green leaves, and some insects. Young poults eat insects almost exclusively.

In improving a woodland for turkeys one must bear in mind the rather large area of flock range and the adverse effect of heavy use for timber on the habitat. The range must be protected from cattle grazing, overuse by deer, and fire. The forest composition should be maintained in types with mast-producing species, and parts of the forest should always be occupied by open forests with hardwood trees of large size. A few large conifers for roosting may be beneficial. Sustained yield (of timber and turkeys) can be accomplished by group selection or clearcutting in small patches. Herbaceous plants and fruit-producing species grow in the openings, and the larger trees provide cover and mast. Special food patches of grain can supplement the winter food supply. Turkeys, once so abundant in the wild forests of colonial days, are just now being nursed back to their rightful place in our forests.

Tree Squirrels

Squirrels have a small home range in a habitat of mature hardwoods or pine-hardwoods composed of some mast-bearing species such as oak, hickory, and walnut. Some old, large trees with hollows for nesting are beneficial, Management practices include: (1) the selection system of regeneration to encourage a continuous cover of large trees of mast-producing species; (2) the elimination of grazing; (3) the reservation of trees which provide needed food and dens for nesting; and (4) the development of cover lanes between wooded areas to facilitate dispersal. Squirrels are entirely forest animals.

Live den trees will provide wildlife shelter and breeding places for many years. For wildlife objectives one or two such trees per acre are desirable.

Beaver

Any small wild stream in a forested or semi-forested area, not in too close proximity to Man's presence, is potential beaver habitat. Beaver are now spreading rapidly over the abandoned farm areas of the rural East. They are persistent dam builders and consumers of trees for food and dam construction. Beaver may be a mixed blessing. They are interesting to watch and they provide pond and marsh habitat for many kinds of wild animal species, including birds and insects. But the flooding and felling of trees often destroy adjacent forests, and an area of deadened timber may not please you. Individual trees within the range of beaver can be protected by a well-maintained and sturdy screen guard. But nothing can protect trees from flooding short of major earth moving or destruction of the beaver dam; and beaver will rebuild a dam very quickly.

At present, beaver have no natural enemies in most places, and if they get completely out of hand you may have to use drastic measures, although laws protect beaver in some states. It all depends on the balance you want to achieve between marshy ponds and forest. Beaver will sometimes build a series of ten or more dams within a mile distance on a single stream. If you do not have beaver on your land, carefully consider the advantages and disadvantages before you introduce them.

Miscellaneous Species

Most other species of forest wildlife fit in the various ecological niches provided by a diversified environment. Both rabbits and quail are well adapted to a mixed farm, field, and forest situation. They use the forest and brushland for cover and obtain much of their food from fields and from grain crops. Woodcock are worm and insect feeders and prefer damp soil and a diversity of tree age classes for cover. Raccoons are forest dwellers that eat mice, fruit, insects, and aquatic animals. Like squirrels they need den trees and prefer a sufficient supply of fresh water. Natural predators such as fox and bobcat need cover and an ample population of prey animals. Non-game wildlife such as songbirds flourish in ecological niches of the same diversified environment suitable for game. The borders between different types of vegetation and cover are particularly good for songbirds. Songbirds are very selective for

This is a green tree reservoir in a pin oak forest in the Midwest. Large areas are flooded in the fall for the use of ducks that dive for the acorns under water. Water is drained off in the spring so the trees will stay alive. The baskets were part of a study to determine the amount of the acorn crop.

particular forest conditions. Some are ground feeders, some trunk feeders, some tree-top feeders, and some feed flying over the forest. The greater the diversity the greater is the number of types and species of birds and the greater is the stability of the environment.

POND MANAGEMENT FOR FISH

The construction of a fish pond is an engineering job. No landowner should make a pond without expert advice and specifications. The Soil Conservation Service of the U.S. Department of Agriculture will inspect your possible sites, recommend a location, draw up specifications for the dam, and advise you on possible contractors to do the job. If you desire a farm pond and have a suitable site, you are eligible for federal financial assistance toward the construction cost. Ask the local Soil Conservation Service or your County Agricultural Agent.

Any dam must meet certain essential requirements. The water outlets must be large enough to meet any expected outflow judged by the area of watershed and the expected maximum rainfall. This drainage is usually handled by a pipe for normal overflow and a slightly higher grassed spillway for emergency flood conditions. For small ponds with small watersheds a spillway alone may suffice. The top of the dam should be well above the spillway level. The pond should have a *minimum* water depth of about eight feet. All these details are spelled out in the specifications. The earth dam must be wedge-shaped, wide at the bottom, and the thickness related to dam height and the soil texture. The soil must have enough clay to prevent leakage and the dam must be sealed at the bottom with some form of "clay plug" or its equivalent. All brush, trees, and trash should be removed from the pond area before flooding. The edges of the pond should drop steeply into the water to prevent pond weeds along the shore. A pond with "feather edges" cannot be managed efficiently for either fish or recreation. Sometimes a narrow dam will hold water but it will be susceptible to muskrat damage. These animals burrow through the dam and thus drain the pond. Heavy mesh galvanized wire placed along the face of the dam will keep out muskrats but the wire is difficult to maintain and if the water level drops muskrats will burrow underneath.

Assuming you have a properly constructed dam, the worst and most likely problem is *pollution*. This can nullify all the time, money, and energy you have spent. The prime criterion for making a decision on locating the pond should be the potential or likelihood of pollution. There must be no intrusion of septic tank effluent, polluted stream water, raw sewage, or barnyard waste. Cattle or pigs must not be allowed access to the edges although it is possible to devise means of limited access for drinking water without pollution. Ponds located in watersheds of heavily fertilized and cultivated fields become overfertile and soon filled with algae, pond weeds, and silt. It is not possible to manage a polluted pond properly for fish and recreation, whether the pollution is silt, nutrients, waste organic matter, or chemicals. In populated areas septic tanks and polluted streams are the worst offenders. In agricultural areas fertilizers, silt, and chemicals such as DDT are most prevalent.

There are no effective direct remedies which will eliminate the effects of pollution. You can spray pond weeds but they will come back. You can use copper sulphate to reduce algae but the effect is only temporary. The *only* way to have an attractive and useful pond is to have it *properly constructed in the first place and to prevent pollution.*

Fish management is a highly technical subject and you should not proceed without expert help. This help can be obtained from the state Conservation Commission or the comparable agency in your state government. Most states raise and distribute fish for stocking ponds and streams. They have certain rules and regulations which must be followed, but if you comply with these regulations you can obtain small fish for stocking free of charge. The species of fish supplied depends somewhat on your personal preference but is limited to fish suitable to the climate and the characteristics of your particular pond.

A managed fish pond must usually start free from all fish except those stocked. Any existing fish should be killed with Rotenone or other substances applied in the correct amounts for the volume of water present and mixed with the water to assure good distribution. It is best to obtain technical help from the agency supplying the fish. Two or three species of fish are supplied to take advantage of the food chain in the pond. Small fish like blue gill eat insects and small plant and animal organisms in the pond. These are called "feeder" fish. Predator fish, like bass, consume the feeder fish. Knowledge about fish management is quite incomplete. All you can do is follow recommendations of your state agency. The most common problem is the great proliferation of small fish such as minnows and bream. They tie up most of the food in a pond and it becomes overpopulated so that none of the fish grow large enough for "keepers." A managed pond should be fished heavily for feeder fish as well as the game fish. Sometimes it is necessary to kill out all the fish and start over, especially if the pond becomes contaminated with rough fish such as minnows and carp. The keys to a good fish pond are correct construction, no pollution, correct fish stocking for the climate and water, and the maintenance of a fish population properly balanced for species, numbers and size.

In a large wild lake with inflowing and outflowing streams predator fish may be stocked, but tight control is impossible and the legal and management aspects are quite different. Dependence should be placed mostly on pollution control, shore improvement, and added nesting and cover material for desired fish. These wild lakes offer the greatest challenge to a fisherman and the greatest rewards to a lover of nature.

THE FUTURE OF WILDLIFE

It is easy to make a case to support the prediction that some types of wildlife will gradually disappear from the earth. Other types such as insects, reptiles, and sludge worms may inherit the earth. Some mammals, birds, and fish at the top of the food chains have already diminished or disappeared. This is a tragic, unforgiveable, and immoral act of Man against Nature. There will no doubt be more and more "game farms" and "shooting reservations" to preserve certain game animals for the sport of shooting. There will also be more and more sophisticated zoos and animal parks. But will there be wildlife as we know it today? Can wildlife withstand the triple sledgehammer blows of pollution, loss of physical habitat, and exploitative killing? Will government agencies and private owners stop the poisoning of the few remaining predators, when the economics of the operation is highly questionable and the immorality certain? Whether or not the present natural types of wildlife can survive will depend on the private and public managers of the forest environment as guided by public pressure. If the

Trout in a clear wooded stream. In recent years many streams which appear relatively clear carry a light load of silt and other pollution.

future Earth is occupied mostly by insects, muskrats, bull frogs, and snakes, it will be our own fault.

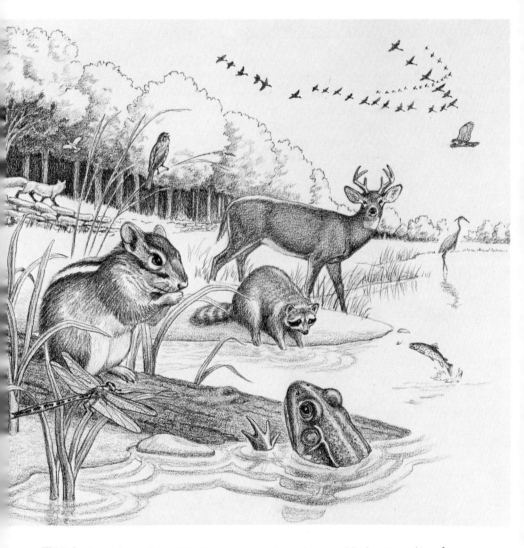

Wildlife is seldom this abundant in one place, but an ideal composite of wildlife and habitat — including forest, field, marshy shore, and water — might look something like this.

7

Recreation and Aesthetics

ECREATION AND AESTHETICS are two three-dollar words meaning fun and beauty. What could be nicer? Can these wonderful things be provided by a forest environment? Yes they can — many kinds of fun and beauty for many different tastes. You can choose your own pleasures and work toward a forest environment that will give you (and your neighbors) these pleasures. Perhaps you want only privacy and a sense of belonging to Nature. Most of us feel this need from time to time. The desire to hunt or fish or to observe wildlife is deeply rooted in many people. The promise of flowering dogwood in the spring and flaming maple in the fall helps us over the dull spots of life. A picnic in the woods by a clear stream is a rare pleasure. The author who wrote, "A jug of wine; a loaf of bread; and thou; in the wilderness," knew something of the deep yearning of man. The bread and the wine and the thou are still plentiful, but the wilderness, or a reasonable substitute, is becoming more and more scarce. Some men obtain deep spiritual satisfaction from a relatively unaltered natural setting of forests, streams, and landscapes. We have freedom of religion and spiritual expression, so Man has a right to Nature's place of worship. You can make your woodland a place of beauty and enjoyment.

RECREATION IN THE FOREST ENVIRONMENT

The forest environment provides all kinds of recreation. Active physical enjoyment carries a large measure of mental relaxation while mental recreation in the forest can hardly be achieved without some use of muscles. Here are some of the more physical things you can enjoy in an ideal woodland area: hunting, fishing, swimming, boating, skiing, archery, skating, tobogganing, sledding, horseback riding, target shooting, and hiking. Activities with greater emphasis on mental relaxation and enjoyment include camping, picnicking, berry picking, maple sugar making, photography, bird watching, Nature study, and just sitting on a stump. This is quite a storehouse of recreational wealth. If you own an area of woodland environment you are richer than you think.

You can consider spending this wealth of recreation in one or more of the following ways: (1) develop as desired for the private use of your family and friends; (2) develop for the betterment and free enjoyment of the local community, including your own family; (3) develop and use primarily for financial gain by charging fees or by leasing the land for particular purposes — these practices are becoming more and more prevalent on lands close to large population centers.

Commercial development for recreation, however, has many pitfalls, and few small woodland owners will want to make this venture. There are perhaps, three possibilities: (1) develop simple, inexpensive facilities to take advantage of the resources present without large investments; (2) make a large investment providing a diversity of high-quality facilities in the expectation of heavy use, large gross receipts, and intensive advertising; and (3) lease the land to others to develop, protect, and operate. This last is the easiest for the owner. Rates may vary from 50 cents per acre per person for hunting small game to $5 or more for waterfowl. It is best to lease to sportsmen's clubs or other organized groups. In this case, the leasing group should be made responsible for controlling trespassers. Land may also be leased to camping groups or recreation clubs for $1-$5 per acre annually. Fees may be charged individuals for campsites, swimming, picnicking, fishing, and hiking on scenic or nature trails. You will need proper insurance to handle possible liability claims. Large commercial recreation developments are big business and beyond the scope of this book.

There are two broad kinds of recreation in a forest environment. One type involves light use where the physical impact of man is hardly felt by the environment. A walk in the woods or bird watching by a few people will not damage the environment.

The author's A-frame in the Catskills. Notice the curved driveway and the power line entrance to the back of the house. The swimming pond blends into the contour of the slope, and the shoreline is well-vegetated. The wild meadow at the upper right and at the front of the house has been kept open by cutting tree sprouts and woody brush to keep them below the browse height for deer. This will avoid "closing in" and will preserve the wide vistas down the mountain and across the valley. The pool is fed by runoff from the mountain slopes, and a spillway is located at the right end.

Special measures to restore or protect the site and vegetation are seldom necessary. But heavy use by hundreds of people actually compacts the soil, destroys forest vegetation, and causes soil erosion to such an extent that the whole environment is altered. In this case, preserving a near-natural environment is an expensive and uphill fight. This situation is most common on camping and picnic areas and on land abused by fire, grazing, poorly executed logging and road building, or some combination of these actions.

With light recreation use, cultural measures to establish and maintain a healthy and diversified environment would include thinning, release, improvement cutting, and group regeneration cutting in the forest as already discussed. These practices will help control the species present, tree size and vigor, and arrangement of age classes in the forest. Such practices fit nicely into the objectives of wildlife production, aesthetics, watershed values, and timber as an important by-product. Construction of nature trails through the forest to various points of interest can be done without damage if the use is light. Simply clear away the brush in the path and the branches that will hit you in the face or body. On sidehills make a "terrace path" about 18 inches wide and firm the shoulders. Leaves will provide a natural mulch and in a few years the path will look like a part of the terrain. Avoid steep paths; go along the sidehill, on the ridges, and in the valleys. Every two or three years it will be necessary to cut back branches to keep the trail clear. Lay the branches flat on the ground well back from the trail and they will soon blend with the forest floor. If you are a nature lover, map the trail for points of interest and designate these points on the trail. Many of your friends will be fascinated by the tree species, a bird's nest, or the home of a raccoon in a den tree.

Private or lightly used picnic or camping areas in a forested area can be constructed without damage to the forest or soil. Choose a level area, with deep soil and large vigorous trees quite far apart. A place in a cove beside a stream is ideal. Place flat rocks on heavily used surfaces and keep a mulch on the forest floor at all times. Do not injure the roots. Most of all treat the trees as *living* things; they react to injury and respond to tender loving care.

Forests which are heavily used for recreation present a much different situation. Soils are compacted, the forest floor litter is destroyed, soil erodes, tree roots are exposed and injured, trunks are hacked, branches are broken, and the trees eventually get sick and die. Some of this is wanton injury, but much of it is simply the result of too many people in contact with the soil and vegetation. This injury can be prevented to a large degree, but it is expensive. The measures required are sometimes called urban silviculture. The chief objective is simply to keep the trees alive and reasonably healthy. The main focus of effort is the soil and the tree roots, but tree species, tree size, and crown size are also important. The soil must be kept intact and permeable to air and water. If this is done roots will not be exposed and injured, and the soil will be well supplied with water and air. Here are some of the things you can do to keep the trees healthy in heavily used areas:

1. Use native species of trees and shrubs well adapted to the climate and the existing soil-site conditions.

2. Keep the forest thinned so trees will develop stocky trunks and long, wide, and full crowns. The spacing between hardwood trees (in feet) should be 2½ to 3 times the diameter breast high (in inches). For example, the spacing between two 12-inch hardwood trees should be 30 to 36 feet from trunk to trunk. With this spacing the crowns will not quite touch.

3. Channel heavy traffic into paths and protect the paths with a thick layer of fine stone (chat) or organic mulch such as wood shavings or coarsely ground tree bark, Such covering must be renewed as needed. Sawdust or straw are not satisfactory.

4. Protect surface areas around picnic tables, campsites, fireplaces, and other areas of severe use with flat stones or some of the mineral mulches. Organic mulches are messy around eating and sleeping areas.

5. Protect trees with natural or planted shrubs along the paths and edges of the heavy use areas so as to give needed protection to the trees. Fences could be used, but they spoil the setting. It is better to use hedges of shrub species native to the area. Some common species are azalea, laurel, rhododendron, hawthorne, holly, sumac, mountain ash, dogwood, redbud, elderberry, and wild rose. These shrubs should not shut in the use areas but rather serve to discourage trampling around the trees.

6. In some cases application of a heavy mulch of forest litter and topsoil is necessary to save a recreation area. But unless future protection is given, or the use load reduced, the area will soon return to its degraded state.

7. The only lasting method of site and tree preservation is to maintain a balance between the use load and the site capacity, as fortified by intensive management. Somewhere in this balance the human users of the environment must accept and understand that trees have life and that life is fragile.

MAINTAINING OPEN WILD FIELDS

Open fields with native grasses, wildflowers, and other plants are commonly included within country property, even though the bulk of the land is forested. It is often desirable to maintain some of these "wild" field areas rather than allowing them to revert to forests over a period of time. Wild fields add greatly to the variety and aesthetic appeal of a property as well as improve the habitat for wildlife. Fields are a place to rest in the sun, pick or admire wildflowers, and gather wild berries. If close to your house, fields also provide vistas and prevent that shut-in feeling usually associated with too many trees too close to a house.

Fields can be maintained in an open condition with a little work each summer. Some fields can be plowed and cultivated, but this is not the answer for wild fields, especially if the land is steep, rough, and rocky. Erosion must be avoided entirely. Smooth fields without too many rocks can be mowed each year and this will tend to maintain a somewhat uniform mixture of grasses at the expense of a greater diversity of flowering plants and shrubs. Mowing will also destroy some nests of birds and small mammals and if done, should be carried out in mid-to-late summer. Mowing may be a partial solution if some portions are mowed every two or three years.

The practice of maintaining a wild field or meadow must include the periodic elimination of all woody stems, though desired flowering or fruit-bearing shrubs may be left to grow until their density begins to diminish the field-like character of the area. Woody species which grow into tall trees (such as maple, oaks, or birch) are the most troublesome. These should be eliminated while they are still small, not more than four or five feet tall with a stem diameter of not more than one-half inch. The first time treated the young trees may be larger than this but subsequent treatments should be made often enough to keep the size small so that removal will be easier.

There are three general ways to eliminate tree sprouts and saplings and other woody plants without damage to the site or to the other vegetation. (For example, if a bulldozer or other heavy machinery is used there would be soil and site damage.) First, simply cut off the stems a few inches above ground level. The hardwood stumps will sprout, and cutting must be repeated every three or four years. This method works particularly well where deer are present. Deer will browse the new shoots, and rodents will eat the bark near the ground line. This provides food for deer and rodents and keeps down the woody sprouts. Sometimes this cutting back every three or four years is all that is required to maintain a wild field. However, species such as aspen which spread by root suckers should usually be killed entirely as described below.

Second, cut back the woody stems and spray the fresh-cut surface with a herbicide such as 2, 4-D or 2, 4, 5-T. This can best be done during spring or late dormant season. The 2, 4, 5-T is more effective, but its use may be restricted under certain conditions. Check with the farm supply store or the county office of the U.S.D.A. Cooperative Extension Service. These herbicides applied to the fresh-cut surfaces will kill the roots of the trees or shrubs and they will not sprout. Used in this way, and according to directions, there will be no significant pollution of the site. In the long run, this is cheaper and easier than cutting alone, but it eliminates any deer browse and may add some danger of pollution if large amounts of herbicide are used.

The third way is to apply the herbicide directly to the plant without cutting. It should be applied to the base of the stems as close to the ground as possible. The herbicide 2, 4, 5-T should be used in an oil solution as directed. The material will penetrate the bark, be transported to the roots, and kill the woody plant entirely. Sometimes 2, 4-D is sprayed in water solution on the foliage. This will kill most of the foliage but usually not the roots. These methods too, will eliminate deer browse and fields will be unsightly for a year or two.

If the area of the field is only a few acres, and if deer are present, the best method of field maintenance is to cut back the woody sprouts every few years as needed. The natural look of the area will be preserved, the wildlife encouraged and protected, and the site given maximum protection. But if woody plants are very numerous, it may be necessary to kill some of the root systems during the initial treatment so that the desired field grasses and flowering wild plants will flourish.

In general, a dense grass plus forb cover will discourage woody plant invasion in at least three ways: (1) the grassy vegetation competes for soil moisture, (2) the dead grass mat in early spring produces severe frost conditions for woody seedlings just above the mat, (3) the grass mat is a good habitat for rodents that girdle tree seedlings. Such wild fields may be kept in dense perennial herbaceous cover with a high proportion of meadow grasses by mowing every two or three years. As I said, mowing should be done in mid-to-late summer to protect nesting birds and animals, but be advised that bee and hornet nests are then at their maximum. People susceptible to bee stings should beware!

AESTHETICS IN THE FOREST ENVIRONMENT

Someone has said that beauty is in the eye of the beholder. The beholder is modern Man who has evolved as *Homo sapiens* through two million years in intimate contact with the natural environment. He has necessarily adapted to that environment; he still harbors some blind allegiance to the rocks, hills, streams, and forests. The natural scenery still fills Man with awe. He finds a sunset, a clear stream, or a forest edge a beautiful thing to behold. In the same way, damaged, polluted, or degraded nature seems ugly to us. It is something that lacks restfulness; it does not correspond with our evolutionary history; it introduces an element of unease and guilt.

Yet, to put it simply, modern Man has defaced much of Nature because he loves ease, material goods, and efficiency more than he loves beauty. Or perhaps he thought he could have these things through technology, and still retain the beauty and awe of Nature, or most of it. Now we know better, and it is a happy thing that our ancient and perhaps instinctive bond to natural beauty is reasserting itself. We really do know the difference between the beautiful and the ugly. We love the land because it has always been our home. We had forgotten this love temporarily in the search for ease and luxury for too many people; we preempted too many of earth's ecological niches, thereby destroying the very environment that gives life meaning and saves us from boredom. Now we must take a new direction.

What has all this to do with your woodland environment? Plenty. Just a stand of trees, any stand, is pleasant to be around. But a healthy forest with a diversity of species, types, tree sizes, and ages, growing on a varied topography, offers a feast of sights and sensations to brighten a Sunday afternoon. A program of planting, release, thinning, and improvement cutting can help enhance this beauty of diversity and range of sights, if needed on

Portion of a small wooded mountain lake in private ownership. This is an artificial lake about forty years old. Note the clear water and well-vegetated shoreline. Fly casting from a canoe in this type of environment is still possible in our increasingly cluttered world.

your woodland. These measures have already been discussed in Chapter 5 but for greater emphasis on aesthetics some additional discussion will be helpful. Planting may be done with a variety of flowering or colorful native shrubs, but the plants must not be planted under the canopy of forest trees. Planting in openings or along forest edges is required, and shrubs must be released if entirely overtopped by other vegetation.

Some of the more common ornamental shrubs have already been mentioned. All require some full sunlight for vigorous growth and blooming, but azalea, laurel, and rhododendron will tolerate the most shade. Holly, dogwood, and redbud are intermediate in tolerance while hawthorne, sumac, and wild rose need nearly full sunlight. Do not plant unless your woodland is deficient in flowering shrubs and unless you are prepared to undertake the care required. It would be better to let Nature do it more slowly. Often these plants are already present and can be encouraged by releasing them from overtopping vegetation. This approach is cheaper and often quicker than planting.

Aside from silvicultural measures to shape the form of the forest environment, what other approaches are appropriate? What about cabins or other structures in the forest area? If you can afford it, consult a landscape architect or at least read the references listed in the Appendix. Your landscape should have a unity and harmony among the topography, trees, and structures. The scenes should have the illusive but not rare quality of blending and be pleasant to behold. Thus, the woodland environment would exemplify a sort of continuous cooperation and friendliness between Man and Nature. In the natural landscape Man is an intruder, but this impression can be virtually eliminated when Man's works seem to be "at home," especially where the site and the structure meet. This involves size of the space, the placement in the space, the shape of the structure, and the texture of its surface. The actual landscape is seldom symmetrical, so the placement of the structures should not be symmetrical. It is often good to have unequal and unlike masses of vegetation or terrain balanced on each side. Any structure should be subordinate to the natural features, or at least not brashly dominant. A feeling of functional purpose and efficient circulation of movement enhances a good design.

Pocket gophers, given a choice, build their homes on a southeast slope near water but away from the flood plain. They receive the warm morning sun but escape the hot afternoon sun, the bitter north and west winds, and the flood waters. Man does not always do as well. Build your summer home or woodland cabin with respectful consideration for the topography, wind and sun, high water, and the view. Would you rather have the morning sun or sunsets? Are cold north and west winds important to you? What is the all-time flood mark of the creek? Are the lake shores eroding away toward your cabin? Do you have a pleasant view or can you create a vista by cutting some vegetation? Can you arrange an outdoor deck that will give you a view and add to the harmony of the structure? Before you build read and *think* about all these things, and more besides. For example, will your sewage system pollute a stream or lake? Developing a beautiful, natural setting is not easy but it is fun.

One final word. Have you ever had that sensation of supreme well-being when your whole body tingles and your mind glows? This is an experience which may be suddenly sensed without warning or produced after long meditation. It is perhaps caused by an acute impact on your senses of the fitness of things — your perception of a happy relationship between yourself and Nature or yourself and the Eternal. It happened to me on a zero winter night in a mountain cabin as I sat beside a roaring wood fire in the fireplace. It happened in October as I leaned against a large rock and watched the sun filter through the shaking yellow aspen leaves. The feeling of beauty is an experience; the potential for this experience lies deep within the ancient nature of Man. Man is happy when he is *in* Nature. Yet we have not always understood this. Wordsworth, in his finest sonnet, laments this human weakness:

> The world is too much with us; late and soon,
> Getting and spending, we lay waste our powers:
> Little we see in Nature that is ours;
> We have given our hearts away, a sordid boon!

8

Protection of Watershed Values

WATERSHED WITH A TIN ROOF would provide the greatest total yield of water downstream, and the water would be clean. But the water runoff would come in spurts alternating with zero yield, and there could be no other values from the watershed. Small paved watersheds are actually used in some tropical areas as a method of collecting water for domestic use. This practice is obviously inefficient for most purposes and in most places in the world. But it does illustrate the problems connected with managing a forested watershed.

We want the watershed land to produce forests or other vegetation, but we also want an ample yield of clean water which flows somewhat evenly. Because of interception and transpiration from leafy surfaces a forest reduces the yield of water in streams. If we were to cut all the forest the total water yield would be increased but it would be more polluted with mineral nutrients and the runoff peaks would usually be higher. Without extreme care in logging there would be great danger of soil erosion and increased silt in streams. An uncut watershed will produce less water yield, but the water will have maximum purity and lower peak flows in the summer. Watershed management depends on the objectives sought. Most owners and communities want some reasonable mix of full watershed protection and water yield and quality which are compatible with desired uses of the forest. Some examples will be given in the following pages.

What you do on your woodland regarding watershed values probably has a greater effect in the larger community than does any other forest practice. The reason for this is clear. Water goes many miles downstream. What happens to the water on your land influences the total downstream area to a greater or lesser extent. Legal regulations regarding runoff and pollution from upstream lands already exist in some areas, and these will almost certainly be strengthened and extended as public pressure mounts. The days when landowners can, with impunity, pollute water with silt and other wastes are numbered. The soil, chemicals, and nutrients are lost, and while being lost, they spoil the water. The sensible watershed management which can prevent this will be discussed briefly in this chapter.

WATERSHED PROTECTION

The overriding fact is that dense vegetation virtually prevents soil erosion. The soil from entirely denuded areas quickly washes down the slopes and into the streams, the lakes, and finally the ocean. This is called accelerated erosion, as distinguished from the very slow geologic erosion which occurs naturally in geologic time on vegetated watersheds. On a bare area a single storm can remove more soil than ten thousand years of geologic erosion. In the Copper Basin of Tennessee acid gases released from copper smelters killed all the vegetation on many square miles of surrounding land. Within just a few years the topsoil and part of the subsoil were eroded away. The area was a badlands of red subsoil. The function of vegetation in holding soil in place and preventing the siltation of streams and lakes is absolutely essential.

How can vegetation protect soil to this extent? In the first place the driving raindrops never hit the soil directly. They hit the leaves, stems, and dead debris and percolate into the soil. This is why runoff from a heavily forested watershed is clear. No soil particles are disturbed or moved. Secondly, the soil is held together by a mass of roots and rootlets, all interconnected to each other and to the strong main stem. The soil is held in a mesh of roots. In addition, soils under forest vegetation have much organic matter, which increases the porosity. Dead tree roots form canals which also increase percolation. Thus, water percolates into these soils with great ease and normally flows slowly down the slope

Raindrops that hit forest litter do not cause erosion. The water is slowed down and percolates gently into the porous forest soil. Deep forest litter also provides a home for small forest animals as well as insects and many other kinds of living things.

under the surface. Part of the water is retained in the soil and part is only detained to be released for many days after a rain. This accounts for the rather steady flow from a forested, as compared to an agricultural, watershed. Sometimes, however, rains are so severe that the whole soil mantle, including the trees and rocks, slides down the hillside. This happened in western Virginia in 1969 when nearly thirty inches of rain fell in one twenty-four hour period. Any time the soil mantle on a well-forested watershed is saturated with water, additional rain will run off into the streams. Even then, however, much of the runoff is subsurface rather than surface flow, and erosion is minimal unless landslides occur on steep mountain slopes. Forests cannot prevent major floods caused by heavy and prolonged rains or rapid melt of heavy snowfalls. A five-inch one-day rain in the headwaters of the Pidgeon River in western North Carolina produced only a moderate stream rise, but saturated the soil mantle. Another five-inch rain the next day produced a major flood, taking out bridges and causing landslides.

Since the prevention of site damage, soil erosion, and stream pollution is an absolutely essential part of intensive forestry practice the question arises, to what extent can the forest be used and still protect the watershed? This depends on the type and condition of the forest, the topography, the soil, and the climate. The key goals of forest practice are (1) to maintain a vegetative barrier between falling rain and bare soil, (2) to retain the root mass in the soil, (3) to preserve the soil structure and (4) to avoid major soil disturbances such as roads, ruts, and ditches, unless properly planned and executed to prevent washing. These goals are hardest to attain on steep slopes with shallow soils. Logging, with the necessary skid trails and roads, can be very damaging. In many cases no logging at all should be permitted. Level land with deep soils, like alluvial lands or the Atlantic Coastal Plains, are much more stable. Some soil types erode more easily than others; loess and other fine-textured soils erode easier than sandy or gravelly soils. Climate — expressed as the intensity, frequency, and kind of precipitation — also strongly affects attainment of the goals. The continental climate of the interior United States is notorious for heavy downpours or "gully washing." Erosion on snow-covered areas is minimal, but in southern latitudes rain beats on the ground the whole year and frost action on bare ground causes slippage down the slope. Soil in cooler climates retains a large amount of organic matter, essential to good percolation, while soil organic matter in warmer climates tends to be oxidized and thus reduced.

What uses or treatments of the forest can degrade it for watershed purposes? These factors are (1) fire, (2) grazing, (3) timber cutting, (4) mechanical site damage, (5) wildlife overpopulation, and (6) overuse by people. Note, however, that damage occurs only after some critical intensity of use is reached, some intensity that will prevent attainment of the four goals stated in the preceding paragraph. But such intensities of use and misuse have been common in the past and are still common today. It is not so much that knowledge is lacking; it is, rather because we do not care enough to apply the knowledge, or the application will lower *short-term* profits. Thus, the watershed may be degraded for perhaps a thousand years to earn additional income today.

The six factors mentioned above tend to be interrelated. Grazing and overuse by people cause soil compaction, destroy the forest floor vegetation, and lead to soil erosion. Fire bares the soil and destroys organic matter in the surface soil. This leads to increased erosion and soil compaction. Fire has also been used to "improve" woodland grazing, and combined fire and grazing year after year can literally destroy the soil on steep slopes. Heavy timber cutting, with careless logging practices (see Chapter 10), can lead to mechanical site damage and resulting erosion and gully formation. Clear streams can be choked with debris and silt in one year. Partial cutting, without other damage, will affect watershed values in no significant way. Clearcutting, without any soil damage, usually will temporarily increase nutrients in the streams but not the silt load. But it is most difficult to clearcut and log without some site damage. Clearcutting, as practiced by an unregulated commercial logger, may be a disaster for watershed values. Repeated clearcutting on steep slopes will eventually degrade the watershed. Some sites with steep slopes and shallow erosive soils should be left undisturbed and retained forever in the natural condition. Although rare, overpopulation of wildlife can damage a watershed through soil compaction, destruction of cover, and soil disturbance. For example, winter deer yards may have a serious effect on local conditions, and continued heavy browsing of brushlands will greatly delay the development of forest conditions.

An outstanding example of serious watershed damage occurred in the high spruce forests of the southern Appalachian Mountains.

After clearcutting the spruce timber, the logging slash and remaining vegetation almost always burned. These were fierce fires which actually consumed most of the organic soil. Heavy rains washed away the remaining loose soil, and in two or three years the watershed was changed from dense forests with a thick mat of wet organic soil to bare rocks, or to ferns and briars on a thin layer of mineral soil. I have seen where two or three feet of organic soil have been lost in a few years. This soil had been developing for tens of thousands of years. Less dramatic but more widespread damage occurs on steep south slopes of eastern hardwood regions. South slopes dry out early in the spring and are subject to burns before "green up" time. If burned, litter and cover are destroyed, erosion occurs, and the watershed is damaged. This type of watershed damage was formerly prevalent in the hilly sections of the Central States, the southern Appalachians, and the Piedmont. Better fire control has now greatly reduced fires.

WATER YIELD

Sometimes the total volume of water runoff from a watershed is important to a community or an industry. This happens when the watershed supplies a stream, a lake, or a reservoir used for a city water supply or for irrigation. In the humid eastern part of the country, volume yield is usually adequate and much less important than the quality of the water.

Water yield has two components: the total annual runoff and the periodicity of the runoff (the high and low peaks). These tend to be affected somewhat differently by vegetative cover. The maximum total yield occurs with the minimum of vegetation, in practice just enough to prevent unacceptable water pollution and site damage. In an extreme case the whole watershed could be "mowed" every few years on sites with gentle slopes and deep soils (but there would be few other values produced). A watershed with minimum vegetation would usually have a greater but more uneven summer runoff. Soil moisture would tend to remain higher, and the soil would have less water storage capacity. Rain falling on a completely saturated soil is like rain on a tin roof: all of it will quickly run off. In actual practice it is probably impossible to maintain minimum vegetation without soil damage and loss of soil structure, which would decrease the percolation rate. At least the margin would be very thin.

In northern climates the vegetation-snow interaction is a factor in peak flood flows. Forest cover tends to retard snow melting, thus postponing runoff to a considerable extent in the spring. But this may be undesirable if melt occurs all at once. Snow melts earlier in cleared openings, and openings in the forest, as in group selection, tend to desynchronize snow melt and thus diminish runoff peaks.

It is possible to maintain forest density at a low acceptable level with scattered openings for regeneration and wildlife. This will increase the water yield as compared to a dense forest without unduly diminishing other water and forest values. Yet, the amount of increased yield by this method is small, perhaps not more than 10-20 percent. If water yield is important, and other forest values including water quality are also important, one solution is to store the water in reservoirs during peak flows in the spring and early summer. Also, before drastic steps are taken to clearcut forested watersheds, the *use* of the water should be carefully checked. Fantastic amounts of water are needlessly wasted; it is even used to flush out polluted streams to save the cost of sewage treatment plants. Clean water and air are no longer free; indeed, they are becoming almost unavailable. As one of millions of woodland owners (and voters) you have a small but vital voice in the future supply.

WATER QUALITY

To most woodland owners in the East, water quality has much greater appeal than water quantity. The quality of water has great impact in evaluating private streams and lakes and those of the local community. However, the kind of water use determines the quality of the goals that must be met. Is the water to be used for drinking, aesthetics, swimming, fishing, irrigation, industry, or a combination of some or all of these? Obviously, some of these uses are compatible. Even industry requires pure water more often than not. Clean, unpolluted water is desired for drinking, aesthetics, and swimming. Fishing is best in clean water, but some fish thrive in muddy water. No fish thrive in water heavily polluted with chemicals or organic sewage. Given a choice, most people want clean water. Clean water can be produced by correct management on all the little watersheds of a stream. Clean water for a community or region can be produced only by the utmost cooperation and regulation.

The cleanest and purest water will be produced on a heavily forested, undisturbed, and uninhabited (by people) watershed with deep porous soil. Anything less than this will be something of a compromise, but, with correct management, the compromise can be acceptable. Heavy habitation, severe fire and grazing, widespread clearcutting and logging, and major site disturbances are unacceptable if unpolluted water is desired. Forest thinning, improvement cutting, release cutting, and single tree and group regeneration cutting are almost always acceptable if roads and skid trails are properly located to minimize erosion. Measures to assure clean water are often the same as measures to obtain other uses on the forest. These measures fit into the multiple use picture. The motivated landowner can push ahead with great vigor along these lines with every assurance of success on his own land. The golden rule for clean water in streams is: Keep intact at all times the thick skin of trees, shrubs, and litter on the soil of the watershed, and especially do not expose bare soil to direct hits of falling raindrops.

9

Harmonious and Integrated Uses

OST FORESTS PRODUCE several values. The usual and best management for small forest ownerships is for integrated (multiple) uses. Uses may be harmonious or even complementary, but some may conflict. For example, a diversified forest is highly desirable for wildlife, recreation, and aesthetics, and diversity is also acceptable for timber. But a dense deer population conflicts with timber because regeneration of desirable tree species may be impeded. A culture of one species, all even-aged, might show the highest profit from timber but have little use for wildlife, recreation, or aesthetics.

This is a very complex subject with many variables and combinations of variables, especially when considering integrated uses on the same area as distinguished from separate single uses on the same forest. Luckily most of the uses are, or can be, made compatible to some degree. You will have to compromise a little here and there, but the sum of the uses may well be greater than any one use, or it may better satisfy your own desires.

Perhaps a good way to give some understanding of harmonious and integrated forest uses is to identify the various factors and characteristics of a forest situation and to show how each is related to uses for timber, wildlife, recreation and aesthetics, and watershed and water. These factors range from ecological characteristics of trees and forests to forest management and ownership patterns. The relationship of each of the four uses to each of twelve important factors is described briefly in the following section. From this you can determine whether or not the uses are reasonably compatible. For example, the optimum species composition would emphasize timber species for timber production, food and shelter species for wildlife, ornamental and hardy species for recreation and aesthetics, and any site-adapted species for watershed and water, recognizing that many of the species overlap for two or more uses.

GUIDE FOR INTEGRATED USES

For each of the twelve selected factors the requirements for timber, wildlife, recreation and aesthetics, and watershed and water are given below.

Species Composition

For timber production you want species which are currently or potentially most valuable for logs, veneer bolts, or, in some cases, pulpwood. The species should have good form and grow well in the climate and on the site. Species favorable to wildlife must provide food, shelter, or both, but many of these are timber species such as oaks, cherry, walnut, hickory, hemlock, cedar, pines, and many others. For wildlife, care would be taken to retain some favorable species. For recreation and aesthetics, hardy ornamental trees are desirable, but many of these are also timber and wildlife species. There would also be greater emphasis on flowering trees (see Chapter 7), but many of these are also useful for wildlife. For watershed protection and water any vigorous and hardy species adapted to the climate and site are suitable. There is no conflict with the other uses. Actually, the natural mix of native eastern hardwoods is suitable for all uses. The manager will want to shift the emphasis a little one way or another to favor certain uses.

Regeneration

For timber and wildlife, regeneration should be prompt, and, as pointed out above, species are important. Browse from forest regeneration is needed for deer, but browsing must not be too

An opening in the forest about five years after cutting to harvest timber and create a space for some regeneration of trees. This is group-selection silviculture, but in application most openings would be much more irregular. A mosaic of openings and tree groups of different ages provides a continuous diversified forest suitable for integrated uses.

severe or trees will not grow normally. Other forms of wildlife use new regeneration, along with the accompanying briars and brushy growth, for food and shelter. But wildlife other than deer seldom seriously damage timber values. Promptness of regeneration is not so important for recreation and aesthetics, but planting and intensive culture to obtain particular species may be used. For watershed and water values, regeneration should be prompt and abundant, but species are not so important if they are adapted to the climate and site.

Growth Rate of Trees

Fast and uniform growth is desired for timber production. This means correct stand density maintained by thinning. For the other uses, growth rate itself is not so important, but fast uniform growth is completely suitable for these uses. There is no conflict except where real wilderness conditions are desired.

Forest Diversity

A highly diversified forest is required for good or even adequate values for wildlife, recreation, and aesthetics. This includes species and age classes of trees. On large areas diversity is also desirable for timber production, and on small areas it is perfectly acceptable but not necessary. Diversity is not necessary for watershed and water in the short run but would be beneficial in the long run because the forests would be more stable.

Forest Density

The optimum density for timber is usually moderate and attained by proper thinning practices to keep the trees in a free-growing condition but with the crowns touching or nearly so. This is not especially detrimental to wildlife, recreation, or aesthetics, but these uses are enhanced by a more variable and diversified density. Low density is more favorable for high water yield and higher density for water quality and watershed protection. But densities favorable for timber are generally satisfactory for all water values.

Tree Quality or Condition

Timber-quality trees are needed for best timber values but can also be desirable for the other uses. In addition, wildlife needs den and cover trees, and trees with eye appeal are desirable for aesthetics. These may not be desirable for timber. Provided that trees are healthy, their quality and form have little effect on water and watershed values.

Silvicultural Systems

For hardwood timber production, suitable silvicultural systems will depend on the condition of the forest. This includes the many factors already discussed in Chapter 5. The silvicultural systems may be clearcutting, group selection, or single tree selection. But for the best wildlife, recreation, and aesthetic values, forest diversity is required, and this is attained by group or single tree selection. Repeated and frequent clearcutting will give the maximum water yield but would eventually cause site damage. Group or single tree selection is the best method for normal water yield with good water quality and minimum erosion and other site damage.

Effects of Intermediate Cutting

Thinning, improvement cutting, and release cutting increase the growth and quality of trees for timber. But, properly done, it also improves food and cover conditions for wildlife, favors desired species and trees for aesthetics, and slightly increases the yield of water. Intermediate treatment is a practice that can be beneficial in many ways.

Logging Methods

For timber extraction the cheapest method of logging is often employed, but for all the other uses, this is almost never permissible. Logging should have a zero or minimum impact on the forest environment unless the non-timber values are to be sacrificed. This is especially important for water quality in streams, aesthetic appeal, and site damage.

Sustained Yield

For timber, periodic or irregular yield over fairly long periods of time is acceptable. Annual yields of wildlife, recreation, and aesthetics are desired and expected. Annual yields and protection are mandatory for water and watersheds.

Costs and Values

Costs and returns for timber are on a dollar basis and relatively easy to compute. Wildlife, recreation, and aesthetics usually have high intangible values, and the dollar costs are justified on the basis of personal and social satisfactions. For water and watersheds, both the dollar and intangible values may be high, and costs are justified on an economic, personal, social, and long-term resource basis.

Small Ownerships

Small owners cannot have sustained yield of timber by extensive clearcutting or other form of quick liquidation. The diversity needed on small tracts for wildlife, recreation, and aesthetics requires some form of selection cutting. Cooperating groups of small owners are needed to influence water yield and quality of larger streams effectively, but small streams can be affected by relatively small forested areas, such as your woodland.

HARMONY OF WILDLIFE, RECREATION, AND AESTHETICS

Of the forest uses discussed above, wildlife, recreation, and aesthetics have the most similar requirements. About the only differences in requirements among these uses are in species, tree quality, and regeneration. Wildlife use emphasizes food and cover species while recreation and aesthetics require some ornamental species. However, some species are common to both uses, and many timber species are also useful to wildlife and for recreation and aesthetics. The same situation applies to regeneration. For deer, there should be greater emphasis on sufficient browse. For recreation and aesthetics, more intensive planting of ornamentals might be justified. Both recreation and aesthetics could well employ timber-quality trees with some emphasis on den and cover trees for wildlife and on unusual trees for aesthetics. So there are no mutually exclusive forest characteristics required for these uses, only a slightly different placement of emphasis. Both require forest diversity, both can be achieved by single tree or group selection silviculture, and both can be adapted to small ownerships.

A mixed upland hardwood forest found in the Appalachian Forest can provide a good example to illustrate the harmony of wildlife, recreation, and aesthetic uses. The chief timber species are red and white oaks, hickories, yellow-poplar, black walnut, ash, basswood, black cherry, black gum, beech, and sugar maple. The other woody species, in a subordinate position in the forest, are dogwood, redbud, hophornbeam, persimmon, sassafras, sumac, service berry, ironwood, and red cedar. The forest has been partially cut twice in the past for sawlogs, but hollow, defective, and other cull trees have been left. The forest is a mosaic patchwork of age classes intimately mixed together. Tree size ranges from large trees of twenty-five to thirty inches in diameter down through smaller sizes of poles and saplings. The forest is highly diversified as to site quality, species, and tree age and size. Many trees are of poor quality or worthless for timber. Fires have been prevalent in the past, and fire scars on tree butts have allowed the entrance of decay fungi, leading to heart rot of trees. Unmerchantable trees left from past logging operations have increased in size, and may have developed hollow butts or holes in the upper trunk where large limbs have died and broken off. Yet many trees of all sizes are good growing stock as described in Chapter 5. Former openings in the forest made by logging or natural tree mortality have filled with new reproduction which is now in the sapling, pole, or small sawtimber stage. Occasionally new openings are present, caused by recent tree mortality. For eastern hardwoods in general, great emphasis must be placed on the wide variation in site quality, even within a single acre. This directly influences species mix, tree height, and diameter and tree condition. Site diversity, more than any other factor, affects forest diversity.

How can this forest be used if your objectives are wildlife, recreation and aesthetics? There are plenty of food and habitat trees for raccoon, squirrels, and turkey, but deer browse is scarce and grouse habitat is not optimum. The forest is varied and interesting. Good locations for nature trails and camp and picnic sites are typically plentiful. But large rotten trees may present a safety

A forest managed for integrated uses. This scene shows improvement cutting on the left leaving the good immature trees to grow. Near the center a group of trees has been harvested, and sapling reproduction is occupying the opening. A large den tree in the foreground, two beautiful white birch in the background, and a hemlock along the stream have been left. Note the piles of brush for wildlife. This is a northern hardwood forest, and trees of yellow-

birch, black cherry, beech, red oak, and sugar maple can be identified. The deer herd should also be managed because too many deer will consume new regeneration of forest trees. When woodlands are interspersed with fields, however, deer find much of their food outside the woodlands. The woodland owner lives in an idealized setting with a pile of wood for the fireplace from the thinnings and the tops of sawlog trees.

hazard. The diversity of species, ages, and tree shapes has high aesthetic value as do the native flowering trees in the understory and at the edges of openings. Fall coloration is enhanced by black gum, red oaks, maple, yellow-poplar, sumac, and dogwood. Red cedar adds a touch of green during the winter. The large, perhaps misshapen, and rotten cull trees may or may not add aesthetic value in your eyes. But when such trees provide the home of wildlife they have a definite appeal. It must be concluded that the forest practices, as already discussed in previous chapters, are easily applicable in this forest. The harmony of these uses fits the ecological facts of our mixed hardwood forest.

INTEGRATION OF TIMBER VALUES

But suppose you also want timber values from your woodland. What do you have to sacrifice in wildlife, recreation, and aesthetics to obtain dollar returns from timber? Or conversely, what do you have to sacrifice in timber returns to assure acceptable wildlife, recreation, and aesthetic values?

The points of conflict between timber on the one hand and wildlife, recreation, and aesthetics on the other are not critical. They can be blunted or eliminated by proper use of silviculture and some adjustments of values received. Forest diversity and timber production can exist side by side if a group selection system of silviculture is used. Groups of mature or low-quality trees would be harvested, leaving openings for regeneration. Many desirable timber species are also useful for the other values. At worst there would be some sacrifice of growing space occupied by special wildlife, cover, and food trees and by ornamental species. There might also be some sacrifice of space occupied by den trees or trees with unusual features. Regenerating timber species is not compatible with an unduly dense deer population. Yet, as we have seen, timber cutting provides greatly increased browse for deer. But the deer must be managed, (kept to proper numbers) to balance the available food supply and habitat. Forest density can have a fairly wide range without serious effects on any of the uses. A variable density from place to place affects timber growth only slightly, and thinning and improvement cutting benefits both timber and wildlife.

Let us look at the typical eastern hardwood forest just

described. How can timber values be obtained here in harmony with wildlife, recreation and aesthetic values? Some compromise is necessary. The cull trees occupy growing space needed for quality timber trees, yet some of the culls may be needed for den and food trees. Eliminate those least valuable for wildlife, but leave two or three per acre of the best den trees. Hickory, walnut, oak, yellow-poplar, cherry, beech, persimmon, dogwood, sumac, and red cedar, among others, all provide wildlife food. Timber objectives, when properly sought, seldom reduce wildlife food and habitat. On the contrary, cutting small openings provides deer browse, edge environment for wildlife, brush for wildlife cover, and sunlight for flowering and food trees like dogwood and persimmon. But timber objectives do suffer in other ways. Time must be spent to lop logging slash for better appearance and quick decay; work is required to fell cull trees rather than kill them and leave the dead trees standing; some game food and flowering trees and shrubs should be eliminated for best regeneration of timber trees in openings; and logging must be carefully done to avoid ugly damage. Yet, all of these compromises can be made with only a little extra planning and expense. But as described in Chapter 10, this is money wisely spent if you desire full use from your woodland. Remember that Nature heals small, shallow wounds in the forest environment very quickly. Great, deep wounds heal only in geologic time.

Perhaps the greatest conflict between timber and other forest uses is concerned with cutting and logging methods and costs and values. Clearcutting large areas is simply not compatible with optimum diversified wildlife production and is a disaster for recreation and aesthetics. For timber production it is desirable to log by the cheapest method, but this is seldom compatible with minimum damage to the forest environment and wildlife habitat. Clearcutting and the cheapest machine logging may increase immediate dollar profits from timber but greatly decrease other values. Therefore, some form of modified cutting and logging will considerably increase the total values from the forest, even though timber profits are decreased. Much depends on the mix of objectives desired by the owner or the general public. On small ownerships it is virtually impossible to have sustained yields and integrated uses with any form of quick timber liquidation. But, by the same token, it is possible to produce timber dollar values without sacrificing much wildlife, recreation, or aesthetic values, as we have seen.

A hardwood forest long managed by the group-selection method. Recent cuts can be seen on the background hillside. The trees growing in groups cut fifteen to twenty years ago are hardly distinguishable at this distance from the surrounding forest. The age classes could be identified within the forest but not at this distance. In the right foreground an opening made about ten

years ago contains sapling reproduction, and several stumps are visible. The
objective has been to maintain a continuous and diversified forest cover
accompanied by proper management of the deer herd to permit forest
regeneration. This is an illustration of integrated uses.

The same hardwood forest area recently clearcut for all sawlog and pulpwood timber products. This area has not yet been "cleaned up" and in actual practice such clean up is often not done. All the standing cull trees and snags down to about two inches in diameter should be felled, and all the live stumps smaller than about twelve inches in diameter should be killed to

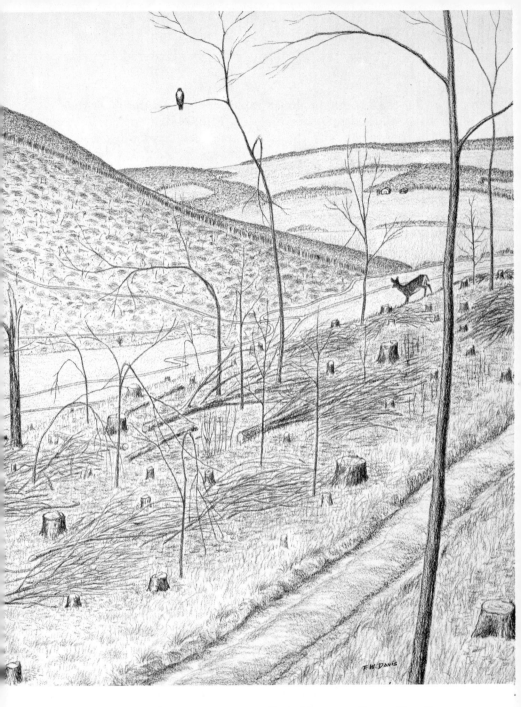

prevent stump sprouts. If stump sprouts are allowed to grow, the quality of the resulting forest for timber will be reduced. If cull trees and snags are left standing they will eventually occupy too high a proportion of the area. This cleaning up after clearcutting may cost $20-40 per acre.

Yet all the timber dollar values are not on the side of clear-cutting. Clearcutting nearly always involves the cutting of many small trees along with the large ones. These have a low value per unit of volume and a high harvesting cost per unit of volume. Cutting small trees returns a low stumpage rate to the owner. Group or single tree selection concentrates on cutting large mature trees where the difference between the cost of harvesting and value of the product is relatively large. This helps to balance the cost advantages of clearcut logging on an area basis. On small woodlands, selection logging of mature trees may actually have an economic advantage, even when other values are not considered.

INTEGRATING WATERSHED AND WATER VALUES

If timber production can be reasonably compatible with wildlife, recreation, and aesthetics what about watershed and water values? The factors which affect watershed protection and water quality can be met by maintaining a continuous forest cover over most of the watershed. This can be done by group or single tree selection cutting and carefully regulated logging to minimize erosion. However, water yield is reduced on a watershed with continuous cover. But if a forest is maintained for other uses, some sacrifice in yield must be accepted. Proper thinning and group cutting for timber and wildlife purposes do increase water yield somewhat, but we should not destroy the forest to obtain the maximum water yield. It is better and more economical in the long run to build reservoirs to store water during winter and spring. There is a direct conflict between water yield and water quality on forested watersheds. Maintaining clearcut watersheds increases water yield, reduces quality, and eventually leads to a damaged watershed.

Except for heavy recreation by many people, the use of forests for wildlife, recreation, or aesthetics has no effect on watershed protection or on water. All uses, however, are adversely affected by the careless commercial logging and cutting practices which have been discussed. The uses on your woodland can be harmonious and integrated if you maintain a continuous diversified forest of species adapted to the climate and site, provide cut openings for regeneration and wildlife, and avoid sudden anti-ecological damage to the site and forest cover.

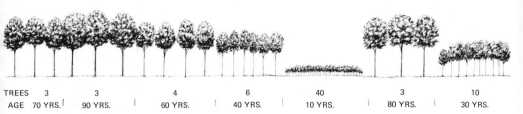

TREES	3	3	4	6	40	3	10
AGE	70 YRS.	90 YRS.	60 YRS.	40 YRS.	10 YRS.	80 YRS.	30 YRS.

A managed group-selection forest would look something like this in profile. This is on a medium to good site where the trees would grow 70 feet tall in 50 years. The original cut openings ranged from 90 to 130 feet in diameter. The tree heights, spacings, and crown widths are in the right proportion according to age and site quality. The horizontal distance is 760 feet, and the tree heights range from 90 feet (age 90) to 16 feet (age 10). This is a random profile through intermingled groups, not clearcut strips. The diagram shows the relative heights of trees of different ages and the amount of space occupied. In an actual forest there would be some understory vegetation. Also, the tree heights within groups would vary more if shade tolerance and growth rate were widely different for the various species.

INTEGRATED USE IN THE SAMPLE WOODLAND

Given the sample woodland described earlier in this chapter, how could you manage it for wholly integrated uses? Suppose your objectives are wildlife, recreation, and aesthetics along with quality sawlogs and veneer logs, strict protection of the watershed, and clean water. What is the general procedure you would follow? The steps are listed below in roughly chronological order. It would be highly desirable to have a forester's help in carrying out the technical procedures.

   1. Make sure you know the boundaries of your woodland and the approximate area in acres. Ideally the boundaries should be marked or designated on the ground.

   2. If the woodland has distinct parts based on site, type of forest, or age of trees, make a rough map showing these parts drawn to scale. Also show major physical features such as ponds, streams, ridges, and trails. A rough map made by pacing, hand compass, and "eyeball" is infinitely better than no map at all.

   3. Make a rough inventory of your forest, giving the number of trees by three-inch diameter classes, species, and tree classes (as described in Chapter 5). On a small woodland this can best be

done by a 100 percent inventory rather than any system of sampling. A visual estimate by an experienced forester is better than blind sampling, especially in the diversified forest we are considering. Species may be grouped based on suitability for various uses. For example, red oaks may be lumped, and flowering trees like dogwood and redbud may be grouped. If the woodland has distinct parts the survey should be made separately for each part.

4. Compute the volume of mature trees and others that might be cut (Chapter 5) to learn whether you can make a stumpage sale for a fair price that would be attractive to a reliable local timber buyer. Here you will need the advice of a forester.

5. In the sample woodland described you would have a salable timber operation of trees *that should be cut* to fulfill an objective of integrated use. The volume would usually be from 1,000 to 2,000 board feet per acre of logs. The essence of good integrated use is marking trees to be cut, recognizing those to be left, and knowing the reasons why. The job is detailed, but the result, after completion of all operations, is a *new, altered,* and *improved forest.* The details of marking will vary, but in our sample woodland the steps might be about as follows:

(a) Designate all those trees down to five inches in diameter that are good timber growing stock, as described in Chapter 5.

(b) Designate den trees and other trees desirable for wildlife, recreation and aesthetics.

(c) Keep in mind that no dogwood or other flowering shrubs or subordinate trees will be cut, except within cut openings where they will interfere with new regeneration. However, such trees at the edges of openings will be left.

(d) The remaining trees will be mature, high-risk, low-quality, or cull trees. Mark among these timber trees for cutting to provide clear openings of about 1/8 to 1/2-acre in size. Occasionally some good growing stock trees may be cut to make adequate openings. This is the harvest cut for timber and to make spaces for regeneration.

(e) Cull trees may be cut or killed, but killed trees will stand dead for many years. They are both unsightly and dangerous. It is better to use them for firewood.

(f) Dense clumps of good growing trees should be thinned to provide adequate growing space. Growing space diameter in feet should be two to three times the tree diameter in inches at breast height. If density of growing stock trees *between openings* does not meet this standard, leave the best mature and low-quality trees to fill in the stand but release subordinate flower-trees whenever possible.

6. Lop all tops so the slash lays close to the ground. Large limbs in tops make excellent firewood.

7. Extreme care must be taken to avoid damage to the site and to the remaining trees. Deep skid ruts up and down slopes are completely unacceptable. Light logging equipment should be used, and logging crews should understand the vital importance of damage. A stiff penalty clause in the sales contract will do wonders in avoiding damage to your forest. Also make it possible to close down the operation at your discretion.

8. There are no good rules regarding species to favor for timber production. As of the mid-1970s, black walnut, black cherry, yellow-poplar, and the oaks are the most valuable for timber in the Appalachian region. In the Northeast, yellow birch and sugar maple should be added to this list. For integrated uses you will want a wide diversity of species adapted to site and climate. Do not worry about the value thirty years from now!

9. Now build the trails, campsites, picnic areas, and other improvements called for by your overall recreation plan (see Chapter 7).

No one ever said that attaining full integrated use is easy. It requires an intensive use of the art of silviculture. Not many foresters have done much of this, but they are becoming more and more sympathetic to the idea. *When woodland owners demand this kind of service, both public and private foresters will provide it.* Most forestry schools have already foreseen such a demand. You, as woodland owners, are in the driver's seat, or at least share it with government and industry.

10

Protecting Your Forest Property

ℐT MAY SEEM that a forest of sturdy trees would be relatively immune to severe or lethal destructive agents, but this is not always the case. Forests through the ages have generally been able to cope with natural and climatic agents but not with Man as he has acted through industrial, agricultural, and social channels. Here I do not mean the necessary clearing of forests for useful purposes but the unnecessary and wasteful practices which destroy or damage forests. I will first review the ways forests can be damaged or destroyed and then discuss some of the effective measures of protection. Below are listed the agents that can damage or destroy your woodland:

Natural agents: diseases, mostly fungal and virus; pathological insects; ecological unfitness, nutrient deficiency and species imbalance to site; and wildlife overpopulation, mostly rodents and ungulates.

Climatic agents: storm damage, ice, wind, and floods; cold and freezing, kill-backs, and frost cracks; fire, lightning fires and extreme fire weather; and drought that kills weakest trees.

Industrial agents: improper logging practices; lack of correct slash disposal; poor cutting practices for the conditions present; land and drainage modifications; and pollution.

Agricultural agents: stock grazing and unproductive and ecologically unfit land clearing.

Social agents: deliberate and careless burning; vandalism and trespass; use impact by people; and use impact by machines, snowmobiles, trail bikes, land rover vehicles.

How serious were these agents in the past and how serious are they now? By far the greatest destructive agents in the past have been improper cutting and logging practices, unnecessary clearing, fire, and grazing by livestock. Over the last hundred years or so these practices have damaged and decimated the forests of America far beyond any reasonable or necessary extent. Fire and grazing have now been largely eliminated as important destructive agents. Progress, though slow, is being made in logging and cutting practices. Clearing for agriculture is still continuing on bottomland soils in response to higher prices for crops and better soil management. Worn-out upland and other infertile and erosive soils have been abandoned from agriculture and are returning to forests at a rapid rate. There is presently a greater movement toward new forests than toward clearing for agriculture.

Insects and diseases have destroyed large areas of over-mature virgin coniferous forests, mostly in the West. But younger, healthier forests are less susceptible. The native insects and diseases seldom reach epidemic proportion in hardwood forests of mixed species and ages in the East. But plantations of one species have been susceptible to both insects and diseases.

The destructive agents now most prevalent in eastern forests have changed somewhat. Improper cutting and logging are still practiced, but added to this is the increasing damage by pollution, land and drainage modifications, and the social agents such as vandalism and use impact. There is no doubt that simple wear and tear on the forest and soil by people will become increasingly important. The misuse of snowmobiles and trail bikes alone could have a profound effect on the forest environment and the wildlife.

CONTROL OF DAMAGING AGENTS

The natural agents can best be controlled by natural means, by silvicultural measures to maintain the forest environment in good ecological health. A diversified forest well-adapted to the climate and site conditions is usually healthy. Insects and diseases are seldom epidemic, and such a complex forest tends to be stable. Forests of this nature can be encouraged by silviculture, as discussed previously.

A simple forest with one species and age class is much more susceptible to insects and disease epidemics. In such cases direct

This is almost ideal stream bank protection. The banks have not eroded because they are protected by rocks and by dense vegetation of laurel, ferns, and other species. This stream margin is a wonderland where air, water, and soil meet.

application of chemical pesticides has sometimes been useful but has short-range benefits and may cause severe pollution of the environment. This has already happened on Earth to a dangerous degree over the last three decades. The mixed hardwood forests of the East are subject to no endemic diseases or insects which reach epidemic proportions. The chestnut tree was eliminated by a disease fungus imported from Europe to which it had no inherited resistance. Also, the elm trees of America are facing extinction from the exotic Dutch elm disease. In both cases foresters and plant scientists up to this time have been helpless. Applying DDT to kill the insect vector of the elm disease has resulted mostly in the death of songbirds.

Other natural ills of the forest are more directly the result of ecological imbalance. Left alone, or intelligently assisted, Nature will adjust to a low soil nutrient level, or the level can be raised somewhat. Sick pine stands usually occur when Man has planted them. In the same way, wildlife overpopulation does not occur except as a response to an imbalance, for example, too much food and too few predators. The case of rabbits in Australia is a classic example. They almost took over the continent and it cost millions of dollars for damage and control. In parts of Pennsylvania deer have prevented for several decades the proper regeneration of forest trees.

With expert advice you may spray urban or ornamental trees for a particular purpose. But first make sure the trouble is not caused by unsuitable environmental conditions. Do not worry about spraying your natural forest of native trees. It will usually be expensive and do more harm than good.

Damage caused by climatic agents is inevitable, but it can be greatly minimized by silvicultural measures in a healthy forest. Stocky trees developed with plenty of growing space are much less susceptible to storm damage, especially windthrow and glaze breakage. Low vigor trees in general are more liable to be damaged by cold and drought. Vigorous trees quickly overgrow damage such as frost cracks and the kill-back of tips. Lightning fires seldom occur in the humid East, but burning conditions sometimes become dangerous in the fall and spring when leaves are down. Most states have a forest fire protection organization and a fire weather warning system. Mostly you will have to depend on the state fire fighting crews, but a neighborhood of alert people can give essential help in reporting fires and in containing small fires until help

Abandoned and eroding old fields can often be protected by planting a suitable species of pine. Pine grows well on poor sites, the roots stabilize the soil, and the pine needle litter protects the surface. This is a successful plantation of loblolly pine ten years after planting.

comes. A small fire can be extinguished quickly by one or two people. An hour later, and after many acres of burn, it may require a ten-man crew with all equipment. Small valuable areas, such as a Christmas tree planting, can be protected by a fire line of bare soil usually constructed and maintained by a bulldozer or plow. But best of all, keep your state fire people informed, and discourage visitors on your woodland during dangerous fire weather.

Careless logging can heavily damage the standing trees left to grow, the reproduction already present, and the soil and site. A skillful and regulated logger can avoid all of these things. There is no need to fell trees against others or to skid logs into standing trees or into patches of reproduction. Log roads and skid trails should be located to avoid rapid water runoff and consequent erosion. Never make a major disturbance straight up and down slopes or along natural water drainages. Water bars and diversion outlets for water may be necessary.

The point is this: If heavy logging is to be done on steep slopes, special measures to avoid site damage *will be required* (see References). Careless clearcutting on steep slopes with shallow soils will cause very great damage. Selection-type cutting on gentle slopes with deep soils will cause little site damage, but the remaining trees can be damaged by careless logging (see Appendix for Timber Sale Contract).

Logging slash is not only unsightly but presents a definite fire hazard during dry fire weather. There is a simple solution for both of these ills. Lop the tops with an axe or chain saw so that the tree limbs lie flat and close to the ground. In this condition the slash stays damp and decays very rapidly. If properly lopped, hardwood slash will virtually disappear in two or three years. Fire hazard will be reduced, appearance will be improved, regeneration will not be impeded, and the soil will be enriched. Slash in large clearcut areas is an especially difficult problem because there is so much of it. In small openings, trees can be felled so that the tops are dispersed, some of them under the canopy of the surrounding forest. If lopped, such scattered slash soon becomes a part of the natural forest environment.

Over long periods unsuitable cutting practices can seriously modify a forest. For example, single tree selection in a forest of moderately intolerant species can change the composition to more tolerant, and perhaps inferior, species. Repeated clearcutting can convert the forest to stump sprouts that are often defective, ill-

This young forest was destroyed by a fire hot enough to kill the living tissue around the base of the trees. The trees subsequently died because they were, in effect, girdled. As trash and litter from the dead trees accumulate on the ground the future fire hazard will be increased.

formed, and multi-stemmed. Or in some cases it can change the composition toward the pioneer species, which may or may not be desirable.

The Catskills region in New York, which has been clearcut two or three times for hardwood acid wood and at least once for hemlock timber and tan bark, is a good example. The hemlock has been virtually eliminated, and the present forest of hardwoods contains a high proportion of trees of stump sprout origin. Where yellow-poplar seed trees were present in the Southern Appalachian and Central regions, this desirable pioneer species often followed heavy cutting. Clearcutting, followed by fire, usually resulted in a drastic change of species from mixed hardwood to aspen, pin cherry, or pine.

Forests close to heavily populated and industrialized urban areas may be subject to air pollution and to drastic changes in land use and drainage patterns. The latter factors may destroy a forest overnight, and the owner can either fight the action or demand compensation. You must remember that local governmental agencies and engineers often seek the cheapest way to build a road or factory — that is, cheapest in the short run. In many cases there are alternative ways that are just as good or better and which do not destroy a desirable forest environment. The climate of public opinion is now favorable for environmental values, and any landowner can expect to receive a sympathetic hearing for grievances, especially if attractive open space is involved.

Air pollution usually damages a forest environment gradually. A few susceptible species like white pine may die or sicken within a few years. Others may live for a long time but slowly become less thrifty. There is no remedy except to stop the pollution. Perhaps the present suffering of humans will force a remedy before there is widespread or serious damage to either people or forests. Trees can be killed quickly by severe air pollution, and owners can sue polluters with a good prospect of success. There are real values involved, and the public is very touchy about air pollution. They reason logically: "Air that kills a tree can also kill me."

Stock grazing is an agent that has damaged woodlands for at least a hundred years in this country. A healthy hardwood forest is simply not compatible with heavy grazing by domestic livestock; forest grazing destroys the woodland and starves the livestock. Livestock compact the soil, expose the roots, eat the tree reproduction, increase soil erosion, and eventually destroy the forest community and its natural values. *So do not allow domestic livestock in your woodland!* It is better to share the cost of a fence.

In this country millions of acres of forests have been cleared for agriculture which were entirely unsuitable for this use. This practice was the rule rather than the exception, and most of that land is now reverting to forests or is being planted with trees. This is now water over the dam, but it is a big and difficult job to manage these natural forests and plantations. Most are growing on sites which have been eroded and depleted by agricultural practices so that the species composition, yield, and quality of the present forest are inferior to the original. The practice of clearing forest land for agriculture is continuing mostly on alluvial flood plains where new techniques make farming more profitable. Do not clear forest land for agriculture until you have consulted your local Soil Conservation Service and other land-use experts, and unless you are willing to sacrifice all the forest values.

The damage and destruction of forests by social agents are now increasing faster than any of the other causes discussed. This is because there are more people, they are more mobile, they have more playthings, and some of them seem to be more careless of the rights of others. Vandalism, trespass, and use impact by people and machines are increasing and will continue to increase for some time. Education may create a majority of decent, careful people who can set a good example to the ever-present careless and mindless minority. This is a vast social problem, and the outcome is questionable. It is certain, however, that many new and stricter laws and regulations must be passed and enforced. It is sad, but more police and more lawsuits will be needed. You must protect your own woodland as best you can.

STEPS IN FOREST PROTECTION

Let us assume that you have a native hardwood forest of mixed species and considerable diversity, something like the one described in Chapter 9. What are the general steps to take in providing protection for your woodland? The following practices would be helpful:

1. Contact your state and local fire control agencies. Determine the extent of their services and let them know your identity, the location of your woodland, and your willingness to cooperate.

2.   Seek advice from your local state forester on the desirability of constructing fire lines around your woodland, plantings, or installations.

3.   Build fences in cooperation with your neighbor if livestock trespass is likely. Do not allow your own stock to go into the woodland.

4.   Legally post your woodland if undesirable trespass is likely. Make arrangements so users will ask permission, or charge fees for various uses.

5.   Keep your forest ecologically healthy by proper silvicultural practices as described in previous chapters. Avoid harsh treatments which quickly and drastically change environmental conditions. The shortcut of chemical protection is usually illusory or even harmful; silvicultural measures are sound and long lasting.

6.   Absolutely prevent site damage and soil erosion through unwise use of machinery and improper logging methods. Keep damage to standing trees and to regeneration at a minimum.

7.   Do not clear your forest land for other purposes unless there is a compelling reason to do so and unless the new use is ecologically sound in terms of soil, topography, climate, and social values. Obtain expert advice before making any such decision.

8.   Remember that native forests have developed over millions of years in a workable harmony with the climatic and site conditions, and even with fire and geologic ice. It is Man who is the "unnatural" enemy of the forest and who can and does destroy forests forever. Even the simple remedies in this book, if followed, would stop this destruction and reverse the trend of the last hundred years.

YOUR DAMAGED WOODLAND — AN EXAMPLE

In the long run bad logging and cutting practices and lack of correct silviculture will probably do more harm to eastern forests than anything else. Yet, the direct, acute, and plainly visible damage is often related to recently emerging social agents such as pollution, vandalism, land modifications, and use impact by machines. You can prevent bad logging and silviculture, and usually you can prevent fire and grazing, but the pressures from people are often difficult to combat.

Let us discuss this from the standpoint of a sample woodland

This forest gully formed at the location of a carelessly placed logging road, a common occurrence unless roads and skid trails are properly located, constructed, and maintained.

This immature but valuable ash tree has been badly damaged by a bulldozer blade. A penalty should be charged for such unnecessary logging damage as shown in the Sample Timber Sale Contract in Appendix B.

easily accessible to people from a large urban area. It could be your woodland. It includes about forty acres of a small watershed characterized by fairly steep slopes reaching to narrow ridge tops and with a small permanent stream in the main valley. One side is bordered by a main graded highway, two sides by farms and open farmland, and the lower side by a suburban housing development on the outskirts of an industrial city. This forest was formerly a jewel of natural environment surrounded by Man's developments and by many people. What has happened to this woodland during the last decade?

The deep road cut along the slope has gradually altered the soil water characteristics just above the road. The cut tends to facilitate flow of water out of the soil mantle, especially along the interface between soil and underlying rocky material. This causes excessive drainage and tends to dry up the soil. Some trees up slope from the road cut have died, especially hemlock and yellow birch, and growth rate and vigor of other trees have been reduced. On the lower side of the woodland toward the housing development, the trouble is too much water. Drainage in this low area had always been slow, but the forest vegetation had adapted with wetness-tolerant species and shallow root systems. The forest was in harmony with site conditions. But the housing development tended to block the drainage patterns, and the water table in the lower portion of the woodland was raised about eight inches. This produced a virtual swamp, killed many of the largest trees, and destroyed the character of the forest.

The prevailing winds carried the smoke and smog from the city industries, and from the houses, across and into the woodland. At first there were no apparent ill effects. Then a browning of the needles of white pine became more and more obvious. Some white pine died, and other trees seemed less green and healthy. Changes were slow and insidious, but even in a decade of time the changes were apparent to a careful observer. But trees have a lifetime of a hundred years or more. What about the long-range effects of constant and perhaps increasing air pollution?

The cultivated farm lands on two sides of the woodland had a significant effect on the woodland. Gullies which had started in the fields extended into the forest, carrying in silt and causing erosion on the forest floor. The small forest stream had become polluted with silt and barnyard organic matter and nitrogen. Several times the weed killing sprays used on the field crops had

A forest of mostly yellow-poplar on a shallow cove site. The forest soil and litter are deep and undisturbed (see next photo).

The same forest site two years after a virtual clearcut of the forest. The skid road was poorly located and excessively used. Several years later a three-foot deep channel was cut by runoff water.

blown into the forest and damaged and killed trees.

The nearby people loved the woodland; in fact they nearly loved it to death. Playing boys, hikers, campers, hunters, and lovers trampled the tree seedlings and ferns, compacted the soil, hacked the trees, and damaged the stream and stream banks. This could have been controlled by limiting the numbers of people, but the *machines* were intolerable. Trail bikes exposed bare soil in an erodable pattern, and the woodland became laced with gullies and potential gullies. Snowmobiles in winter bent and broke seedling and sapling tree regeneration, especially in forest openings where they were needed most. The noisy machinery frightened all forms of wildlife and drove much of it away from the woodland. It also bothered the serenity of the woodland owner, who lived nearby.

Of course, few woodlands would be subject to all these damaging agents, but this is what can happen to a forest in close proximity to many people and their works. To fully protect such forests the owners must have help from governmental agencies and from society as a whole. The owners cannot do it alone.

11

The Challenge of Woodland Ownership

OST SPECIES OF ANIMALS have a strong feeling or instinct for territorial rights and take pains to stake out their home range or even fight for it. Man is no exception. He has a deep-seated desire to own or control land. Man has fought bloody wars to retain territory and the resources of the land. In our modern, increasingly synthetic, and contrived environment the ownership and *use* of some natural land environment gives most men a sensation of having roots, of belonging to the natural scheme of things. It is a good feeling, especially when the land is managed and improved to use and enjoy by both you and your neighbors.

Nowadays there is no need to cite incentives for owning land. Demand for land, including woodlands, is increasing and prices are going up steadily. Land is a hedge against inflation; properly managed it produces economic returns; and it satisfies the deepdown desires just mentioned. All this is evident in the rapidly changing patterns of woodland ownership in the East. About three-fourths of the forest land is included in private, nonindustrial holdings. Formerly most of these woodlands were a part of producing farms, but now over half are owned by non-farmers such as businessmen and professional people. This trend is continuing, and it changes the whole forestry picture because many of the new class of owners are interested in other forest values besides timber, and they have an active interest in obtaining and enjoying these values.

Whether you already own forest land, or are looking for land

155

to buy, the information and concepts in this chapter will at least sharpen your perception and help you ask the right questions. There are three general aspects of ownership you should think about. One is concerned with the physical and biological elements such as topography, soils, water, former land use, and the forest itself. In this connection aerial photographs are invaluable. Another element is economic and social and is concerned with accessibility, transportation, the purchase price of the property, markets, and available conveniences and social services. The legal and political elements include purchase procedure, financing, insurance, possible future developments on the land, zoning, mineral and water rights, and taxes. I will outline some general principles, but unless you have had wide experience you should depend heavily on legal and banking advice to assure a sound and safe investment. You should also seek advice from the local office of the Soil Conservation Service, the State Service Forester, the State Extension Forester, the State Land Grant College, or a private consultant (see Appendix A). However, keep your own objectives firmly in mind, and do not be unduly swayed by particular points of view from any one source. Seldom will all of these people agree.

WHAT IS A GOOD BUY?

The land you buy will depend first on your objectives. Do you want a trout stream, a scenic building lot, a wildlife habitat, a forest of good timber, a land investment, or some combination of these and other uses? You will never get exactly what you want, but you should at least have a goal to work toward. Then you can compromise here and there as necessary. In any event, your objectives will have a profound effect on what land you buy. Here I will assume your objectives are integrated or multiple use, including timber, wildlife, recreation, aesthetics, and watershed values. Below are listed some of the things which determine to what extent your land purchase was, or will be, a good buy. Remember, only you are the final judge, and one point of personal preference or sentimental attachment can tip the scales all the way, regardless of other criteria. I have listed these criteria in order of importance according to my own priority. Yours may be different.

Diversity of Forests and Topography

It is hardly possible to have a variety of forest values and integrated uses without diversity of the environment. Diversity enhances the aesthetics and health of the forest environment and forms the basis of effective management for recreation and wildlife. At the same time it is not a disadvantage for timber and watershed values.

Costs and Opportunity

A bargain is a bargain and an opportunity lost is lost forever. With the growing scarcity of open-space lands and their increasing costs you may well sacrifice other desires to snap up some bargain or rare opportunity. However, unless the purchase is purely for speculation, your other minimum desires must be met.

Future Developments

Take a good look at the future chances for pollution, people, roads, power lines, real estate developments, zoning, other encroachments, and high taxes. If purchase is for speculation, you may not mind some of these things, but if purchase is for your personal use and enjoyment, any or all of these developments could utterly defeat you. In the last two decades such personal defeats have been common and are increasing. Probably there are few guaranteed hiding places, but the chance of another twenty to thirty years of relative peace and quiet still exists in some places. By then we may have learned a new life style, and present trends may have reversed. The dollar value is likely to increase in any event, so in that sense your heirs can "win" in any case.

Presence of Streams or Lakes

For many people this characteristic would be placed first. Indeed, it is implied under the idea of diversity. Water provides recreation and scenic values and greatly increases the value (and cost) of any forest property. With the absence of natural water bodies suitable places to build impoundments are most desirable and commonly used. For a summer vacation home, water for swimming is virtually a must, and water for domestic use is required. Also, a scenic view may be the prime consideration in land purchase.

Accessibility

Your woodland area must be accessible for the uses you desire. Accessibility may range from an automobile road to a foot trail or water route. It is not always the existing access facilities that are important but the opportunity and ease of establishing access routes of various kinds. To some people, easy access to their property is a liability; they want solitude in big chunks. Others want auto access but subdued to the point that tourist and Sunday drivers will never notice the roads. Still others (the majority) want direct access from highways or well-kept country roads. For our integrated use objective there must be existing or potential access by road or truck trail during at least part of the year. Good roads need not be directly adjacent to your woodland, but temporary entrance and exit by light logging machinery or horses, and easy access by foot, are essential. If your property does not have access to a legal right-of-way you must secure one through an adjacent property before you purchase. Accessibility is one of the most important factors in determining the cost and future resale value of land. Often you can buy an inaccessible area at an apparent bargain. Make sure it really is a bargain.

Productivity

Soil, topography, and climate help determine the productivity of the forest in terms of timber, wildlife, recreation, aesthetics, and watershed values. Productivity is the capacity to produce the things you want. A highly productive area not only produces more goods and services but is easier to manage and less subject to damage. Also, it usually costs more. But high productivity is not necessary for a successful woodland operation or a happy ownership experience. Some areas may have high aesthetic value but low productivity for timber. But for successful integrated uses the area must be able to support a healthy, reasonably vigorous forest. Such forests occur on the lower and more gentle slopes, in coves and alluvial areas along streams, and on upland terraces and flats. Steep, rocky mountain sides with thin soils are not productive for timber or integrated uses, but they may have high aesthetic appeal.

Forest Condition and Past Treatment

A forest of good-quality pole or sawtimber-sized trees is a distinct economic advantage and can serve as a base for manipulation to obtain integrated uses. A forest of medium to large trees means that Nature has presented you with a gift of forty to a hundred years — a ready-made factory for the production of all those values already mentioned. For timber objectives the forest condition would rank much higher in my list. Assuming that your woodland has a reasonable cover of trees, their quality for timber is not so important for the non-timber uses. Obviously, land with a forest is greatly preferable to bare land where you start from zero. Also important is the condition of the site as determined by past use. Be wary of land with evidence of severe fires, grazing, erosion, or other site damage. Such damage may require decades to heal and in some cases is irreversible. Such a forest is not only unproductive it is also ugly.

Markets for Goods and Services

Management for integrated forest uses does require at least minimum markets for timber products. An opportunity for recreation-use fees is also highly desirable. Without timber markets, management for other uses can still proceed, but with some financial sacrifices.

Social Services and Conveniences

This might appear first on your list if the area is to be your permanent home. Schools, shopping, cultural and entertainment centers, and the amenities of life would be essential. This is a personal and family value-laden judgment.

Presence of Buildings

A house to be remodeled or a barn to be fixed up may make all the difference in your desire to buy a property, especially if a second or a permanent home is desired. In such cases the house may be paramount and the land and forests gradually managed as time and money are available.

The elements of a "good buy" are many and varied. You

should not neglect the solid attributes of the land, the forest, and economics, but in the last analysis your personal preference, aesthetic considerations, and convenience will often determine the choice. A sense of satisfaction is the chief reward for owning a forested property. You are the judge.

Size of Ownership

The size of land ownership should be determined by your objectives, what you can afford, and what amount is for sale. There is no magic best size. If timber is to be the main product and dollar returns your chief goal, tract size should be at least five hundred acres. Only then is there a good chance of showing a profit from timber alone. As already discussed, timber alone cannot be profitable on land purchased at the high prices so common in the East.

If your objectives are mainly aesthetics, wildlife, and recreation, small tracts, even down to five and ten acres, will serve very well. Many small tracts of just a few acres provide an abundance of forests and wildlife for family enjoyment. With like-minded neighbors hundreds of acres can be joined to form a diversified and lively natural environment. If properly planned, such areas could eliminate the "fringe blight" so common around American cities. The alternatives are easements or public acquisition of lands to form green belts around population centers.

The most common objective of woodland owners is integrated use for the timber and non-timber values we have discussed. This can be obtained on woodlands as small as fifteen acres, especially if other woodland tracts are in the same locality. Wildlife can find a home, recreation of various sorts can be developed, and aesthetics can fill a whole Sunday afternoon of nature watching. A normal forest stand of fifteen acres will grow about 3,000 board feet of timber per year so that 30,000 board feet could be selected and cut every ten years or a smaller amount at shorter intervals. This cut would be attractive to a small logger. You do not need a large forest to practice integrated uses for your pleasure and profit.

FINANCIAL AND LEGAL CONSIDERATIONS

The overriding and all-important recommendation is that you

should *consult your attorney and your banker* before undertaking and completing any purchase of woodland or farm property. An experienced real estate agent, recommended or known personally to you, can be helpful in locating various properties for sale. In addition to the basic items already discussed you must have a clear title, and you must know the status of zoning and of mineral rights. In some states mineral rights are held by some past owner, perhaps a corporation. Do not buy land for multiple-use purposes, or any use except timber alone, unless the deed includes the mineral rights. It is not that you necessarily want the minerals but that you do not want your property torn up by a mining operation. This has happened!

The costs of owning property are (1) the original outlay, (2) interest on the investment, (3) taxes, (4) protection, and (5) management. Your original outlay includes not only the purchase price but all the fees connected with the transaction. Ask your lawyer to prepare a statement of all costs. The original outlay should also include your own travel and other incidental expenses. You should consider how you could recoup the investment and whether you can ever recover it in economic terms. Land purchased in the past has usually paid for itself through inflation and its increase in real value. This will probably continue in the long run but not necessarily in a continuous upward direction. Another way to ease the initial outlay is to partially or completely liquidate the timber. Correct silvicultural treatments yielding timber returns may enhance and improve the woodland, but cashing in timber to pay for a woodland is seldom adequate for the outlay and usually undesirable. Most owners want a living, diversified forest. The long-term growth and increase in value of the timber alone will not usually repay the present inflated land prices and the interest on the investment. Realistically, you will need some *personal capital* to manage a land purchase with any degree of comfort and peace of mind. Assume that you are buying enjoyment and personal well-being, as well as a woodland, as was discussed in Chapter 4.

When money is borrowed to buy land there is no question that interest is a cost of ownership. When personal capital is used, some people forget about interest. In a sense this is natural as we tend to balance it against the joys received and call it money well used. As always, you pay your money and take your choice. Still, interest is a cost of ownership. If you can forget it (except at income tax time) you are a lucky owner.

Taxes are something else! They cannot be ignored. Forest real estate taxation varies greatly from state to state and even for different counties. There may be "yield" taxes, "deferred" taxes, or special assessments. Or forest land may be taxed annually just as other real estate. Forests have been given special consideration by some states to avoid penalizing good forestry practices that increase value of the timber, as distinguished from the land itself. The idea is to tax the timber when it is harvested.

Then there is the added complication of what basis to use for assessment of forest land value. There are three general points of view: (1) basis of actual present use, (2) basis of present market value of land, and (3) basis of forest productivity. You can see what a very great difference this could make in your assessment. Land assessed for market value near cities must often be sold to developers to avoid the ruin of the owner from excessive taxation. States interested in green belts and unspoiled suburban environments use actual present use or productivity as a tax base. In some cases "scenic easements" have been used to avoid fringe blight around cities. The forest tax situation is very complicated, and you should consult a tax lawyer before you buy, especially if your land is near heavily populated areas.

A tip is needed on death and taxes. Inheritance taxes or an improperly drawn will can cause the liquidation of a forest at the death of the owner. It would be ironic indeed, if after many years of investment and loving care, a forest must be sold and perhaps liquidated to settle the estate. There are legal ways to avoid this possibility. Doing so is both in the public interest and the interest of your family. Go quickly to your lawyer!

Protecting your forest involves a cost of ownership and is discussed in Chapters 3 and 10. For your own protection you need liability insurance as protection against claims resulting from accidents on your land. In some states owners are not liable for accidents when permission to go on land has not been granted. Liability insurance can be obtained separately or as part of a package of ordinary homeowner's insurance.

Management involves costs of ownership, or, more precisely, it does so if any management practices are undertaken. A discussion of the ecological, silvicultural, and economic aspects of woodland management is the chief content of this book. But a brief summary of principles and concepts for management policy are outlined below.

WOODLAND MANAGEMENT POLICY

You must make the final decisions on what to do in your woodland. This book is written to give you help and, as shown in the Appendix, a great deal of other help is available. Briefly, you will need to choose your woodland objectives and then make some kind of a formal or informal, mental or written, management plan. In other words, decide specific measures that should be taken and when. The key virtues of such a plan should be simplicity and flexibility. The plan must change with circumstances and needs. Even your objectives may change. Nothing is more certain than change, and a rigid plan will serve you poorly. So update your plan at least every five years. For example, suppose your children will reach swimming and fishing age in about four or five years and you do not have a water impoundment in your original plan. Or suppose the state stocked your area with wild turkey where they had been absent previously. Modifications must be made to adapt to ever-changing conditions.

A forest can be regarded as a "factory" which produces goods and services. There are natural inputs such as sunshine, water, and soil, and there are artificial inputs such as planning, labor, and machine work. How the inputs help to produce the outputs we seek is the chief subject of this book. The *intensity* of forestry practice (inputs) should be determined by the richness, diversity and quantity of the objectives (outputs) desired, while at the same time maintaining the health and stability of the forest ecosystem.

12

Forests of the Future

*T*HE FORESTS OF THE FUTURE will be determined by the goals and life style finally chosen by the people of this country. I have already discussed the functions of forests in our society, and it is clear that our objectives determine the kind of forest practices followed. We have discussed intensity of forest culture (silviculture), the ecological considerations, the relations between forests and a desirable natural environment, and the material and financial aspects of forests and forestry. It would be an oversimplification to say that future objectives will determine the nature of future forests. Let me approach this from the viewpoint of two different scenarios of the future. One future world would be one where Man has reached a harmony with Nature and evolved a life style where materialism is only incidental to the good life. The other world of the future would be a logical and accelerated extension of the industrial revolution; the dominance of present materialistic values; the primacy of the gross national product and its continued growth; and the increasing emphasis on the producer-consumer economy in a materialistic value system. The way we go will in large part determine the nature of future forests and forestry, but probably neither of the models will represent the true future. Probably something in between will prevail, if some substantial change occurs to weaken the present population-consumption-materialism-pollution syndrome. In any event, two scenarios will illustrate a principle by showing the extremes.

First, however, let us look at how things once were, perhaps as seen through the golden haze of innocent boyhood.

RECOLLECTIONS OF CHILDHOOD

On the giant room-sized map of New York State at the 1965 World's Fair, there it was — Acidalia! But I knew it no longer existed except as two old houses and in the memory of a few people like myself who visited there or lived nearby. As a boy, I visited my uncle and aunt in Acidalia nearly every summer from about 1911 to 1922. At age six, my idea of Acidalia was "the best place in the world." At that time, it consisted of my Uncle Blake Calkin's farm house and barns, a post office and store combination, a dozen or so houses, a large horse barn, and a recently abandoned wood-distillation plant.

Acidalia was located in a narrow valley between two mountain ridges in the Catskills. About fifty years earlier, when Uncle Jimmy Brown had first come to Basket Valley to homestead, the valley floor was a dense forest of giant hemlock where it was twilight at noon and nearly dark after the sun dropped behind the mountain in late afternoon. The valley floor was cleared for meadows and crops, and some of the lower slopes cleared of hardwood trees for wild pasture. The beech, birch, maple, ash, and cherry hardwood forests on the mountains were cut two or three times for "acid wood" for the wood-distillation plants in the valley. Most of the hemlock had been cut for barn timbers and tanbark. These forest areas have now regrown again to forests of moderately large trees, and the old logging roads make beautiful and convenient hiking trails. The road up the mountain from behind the old store-place, except for the size of the trees, is just as I remember it as a boy.

Through World War I, and even for about a decade afterwards, Acidalia and the surrounding country were devoted to dairy and sheep farming and timbering. The cool climate and rocky, steep land were suitable only for meadow, pasture, and small grains — mostly buckwheat, rye, and oats. Some of my earliest recollections include the tinkle of cowbells and the baa-baaing of sheep. Buckwheat and rye were made into flour for home use, and oats were fed to horses. For cash crops, my uncle sold butter, lambs, veal calves, wool, and eggs.

My uncle's house was on the valley floor within a hundred yards of the old acid plant, and the lingering smell of the charcoal and wood distillates was present for decades after all evidence of the plant, except an old boiler, had disappeared. In later years, grass grew over the site. Just across the grassy flat and the footbridge over Basket Creek, was the combined general store and post office. This is where I ran errands for my aunt, bought candy, and listened to the tall stories of the timbermen and farmers who always seemed to be present. It was the social gathering place of the community, and I jumped at any excuse to go there. The building was abandoned and torn down during the summer of 1966.

Just down the road from the post office was a stone and timber horse barn. The stone foundation is still there. I loved to watch the feeding of the giant draft horses and climb over the big wagons used to haul cordwood for the factory.

The abandonment of the farms in the valley started in the early thirties. Farming in the Catskill hills could not cope with the Great Depression and the more efficient farming operations down in Orange County, in Jersey, and in the Midwest. "City people" gradually bought up the property for an entirely different purpose — to enjoy the summer beauty and solitude of the countryside. When I returned as a young man just out of college, many of the pastures and meadows had already started to grow up into brush and trees. None of Uncle Blake's cow pastures and only small remnants of the large sheep pasture were still open in 1974. It is all forested to young timber. The valley floor was converted from meadow to pasture, but even this is now mostly grown up to woody brush.

My uncle's farm consisted of a large farmhouse, a cow barn, a sheep barn, a horse barn, a pig house, a calf house, chicken coops, and a wonderful milk house with a cold spring that formed a small stream as it emerged through the foundation. All are now gone or in disuse. This was a good and full life for the people who lived here, and, to me, it is a very sad thing that time has erased this picture. I can hardly reconcile myself to the inevitable changes that have occurred.

Across the road from my uncle's house was the "Smithy." Each summer this house was occupied by that wonderful Smith family from Kentucky — the parents and one older boy and four girls. Life fairly sparkled and snapped when they were there for the summer. The house is now gone. Nearby was a small rough summer house we called the "palace." It *was* a palace during the beautiful cool summers there in the valley. Strangely enough, it still stands and may again give joy to vacationers with a little imagination.

I can, however, recapture in my imagination the ghost of these former days. Better yet, some of the real substance is still there. The smell and feel of the air in the evening, the smell of the sweet-fern, the moist coolness of the forest; these pleasures are still there after more than fifty years! So are the quick running brooks, the forested mountains, and the full moon as it hangs over the mountain top. The winding dirt road up the brook; covered by a canopy of maple, birch, and hemlock, is just as I remember it. The farmsteads and many of the wonderful people are gone, but Nature heals. A new invasion of people is occurring. Their purpose is not work but fun and recreation. Perhaps some wish to recapture the beauty and peace of the valley.

The joys of life were made up of simple things. I recall rising early, milking cows, and then driving them across the narrow valley to the rocky pasture on the other side. They were always eager to go. After breakfast I turned the crank of the cream separator and, later, perhaps the grindstone wheel to sharpen the mowing machine knives. Harnessing the horses for the day's work in the hayfield was a special accomplishment because I was hardly big enough but managed to do it anyway. The greatest feeling of power I had as a boy was to drive the horses up the grade to the cow barn with a big load of hay. How the horses pulled and lunged, and how the load rocked from side to side over the rocky road!

Even a simpler joy was driving the team to church on a quiet Sunday morning, through the woods and past the farms and meadows. The stillness and coolness of the church at Fremont Center pleased me even as a boy. The church is still there and looks the same. My grandmother's name on one of the windows and her grave behind the church is a link with the distant past, when I can remember her comfortable lap.

Sometimes on the way home from church my Uncle Blake would stop the team, go into the woods, and cut a strip of sweet birch bark for me to chew. In retrospect, this was better than candy.

The watering troughs along the road running with clear cold water were stopping places for the refreshment of both people and horses. I can remember how the horses plunged their noses into the water and how we drank from the pipe leading in. It is easy to understand the feelings of the poet who wrote "The Old Oaken Bucket." It was pure joy for a thirsty boy.

At about 4 o'clock in the morning, I was often awakened momentarily by my uncle pushing the milk cart past my bedroom window to the barn. Then I could sleep until five! The thought of milking is always associated with cows that kick and tails that swat you across the face. The cats always had a dish of warm milk, and "new kids" got squirted in the face with a stream of milk from a cow's teat.

Uncle Blake cut and stored hay from early July to late August. Haying was hard work in those days. We had horse-drawn mowing machines, rakes, and hay forks, but the hay was handled loose and much of the work was done by hand. But the summers were cool and the only real hot job was "mowing away"; that is, pulling and shoving the hay to the back corners of the loft so the barn could be filled. As a boy, I could "rake after" — rake up the loose hay left by the men who pitched the hay on the load. I was proud, indeed, when I grew strong enough to pitch forkfulls of hay myself.

At about 4 o'clock in the afternoon, I left the hayfields to bring in the cows for the evening milking. This was my favorite chore — walking up the cow paths among the sweet fern and rocks on the shady side of the mountain. Soon the cow bells would lead me to the herd where I would gather and count them. Once started, they would head down the mountain toward the barn.

My uncle's fences were none too good (there were miles of fence), and sometimes the cows would go out of the pasture into the woods toward the top of the mountain. Then I would strike out over the wooded mountain hoping to hear the cow bells. On those nights, milking was late and cows were sometimes temporarily lost. If a cow had her calf in the big wild pasture or in the woods, she would leave it hidden until she returned the next day. Once I secretly followed a cow until she led me to her calf.

Fishing and "creek watching" were favorite pastimes during leisure hours. Basket Creek was then well populated with brook trout, and their swift flash in the pool bottom was always a thrill. Just watching and listening to the swift water over the bright colored rocks was a boyhood dream world. I still do it, but too many of the illusions are gone. It is not always easy to recapture past enchantment. Basket Creek is still there and still runs swiftly on as it did fifty years ago. May it go on unspoiled forever!

Eating is a joy to most active boys, and I still savor the smell of the big kitchen, with farm gear on the back wall and the pantry where the bread, cake, and doughnuts were kept in wooden kegs. The tastes and smells are unforgettable — dried apples, wild strawberries, buckwheat cakes, maple syrup, salt pork, new potatoes, fresh peas, and corn meal mush with maple syrup on Sunday night. There were usually ten to twelve people at the table in the summer, and no one ever went hungry there.

Helping my maiden aunt gather eggs and finding hidden nests in the barn were hours of sheer boyish delight. Yes, these were boyhood days of joy which cannot be told or written. Acidalia as it was to me then cannot be restored. But we must restore, maintain, and improve the natural features which make these places a source of enjoyment and soul healing. Men require sources of beauty, dignity, and strength. This valley and the surrounding countryside can fulfill these needs or it can become a tawdry rural slum. We can have it either way.

Now let us take an imaginary trip into the future to see, perhaps, two extremes of how things can turn out.

SCENARIO I — MAN vs. NATURE

The year was 2050 in southeastern New York about fifty miles northwest of Manhattan Island. The whole region, including all of Orange County, is densely populated, an extension of metropolitan New York City. The rolling landscape had been intensively urbanized during the previous seventy-five years; houses, apartments, shopping centers, factories, streets, highways, and playing fields have virtually preempted the land. Open space with fields and woodlands is scarce and fast disappearing. People are occupied with daily existence in a Man-made environment, an asphalt and plastic world, an "ant hill" type of society. Food and shelter are adequate but men's lives are sharply constrained by seemingly necessary political regulations and the overwhelming pressure of people and material possessions. Solitude in a quiet local woodland or field is unknown; there is no hiding place in nature for Earth's dominant species, either here or anywhere. Men have been conditioned to value material wealth and creature comforts above all.

The land holdings of the Wood and Fiber Corporation might be considered a typical managed forest. This company owns nearly half a million acres of land in the Catskill and Allegheny regions — land too steep and rough for development of agriculture, though dams, powerlines, and roads intrude heavily on the forests. The company policy is to grow small trees for fiber and for laminated and other processed wood products. Trees are grown on a short rotation, seldom larger than eight inches in diameter, and all trees clearcut in large blocks. For greatest efficiency, yield, and profits all trees are of the same species and age; that is, the forests are monocultures. Forestry practice for wood and fiber is very intensive. Regeneration is obtained quickly from sprouts or by planting with trees of superior genetic strains. These plantations are fertilized and cultured intensively. Insects and diseases are prevalent and heavy spraying with pesticides is routine. Serious and uncontrolled epidemics of insects and diseases sometimes cause heavy losses.

Harvesting is done with heavy machinery, rather like a tree mowing process which removes the entire tree; trunk, branches, and twigs. This is a very efficient method of harvesting, but continuous and repeated cutting has increased erosion of the soil on slopes and has gradually lowered the timber production over the years. Foresters have noticed this, but there is a pressing need for wood and the company policy calls for a speed-up in production to meet the demands and help provide jobs for an increasing population.

Forests are handled like a field of corn. Diversity is minimized and wood yield maximized, at least in the short run. Game and other wildlife are scarce or absent. The habitat is unsuitable for wildlife, and most game is kept in shooting reservations. People cannot afford to sacrifice wood production for aesthetics, and most recreation is organized on playing fields or for spectators in stadia. A Sunday afternoon walk on a woodland nature trail is something you read about in Grandma's old books. Runoff from watersheds is high, and silt and pollution are removed artificially for drinking water. Engineering methods are used to stop deep gullies and possible land slides.

Wood is chipped or cut into small bolts and shipped by truck to the processing plant to make paper, paper board, fiberboards of various kinds, and laminated products. Wood is seldom used in the natural state except for luxury furniture, expensive paneling, and various gadgets.

A company forester inspecting the cutting operations was often depressed. The noise of the harvesting machine gave him a headache, and his mind was uneasy. Recently he had picked up an ancient book by an author named Thoreau, who was obviously a little crazy. Looking around him the forester wondered how

Thoreau could have any such feelings about the forest as expressed in his book. Yet the writing in the book seemed clear enough. Was the forester missing something? Was everybody missing something? Those old-time forests may have been pleasant but the people need this wood and we are already running behind. He shrugged and walked toward the tree-mowing machine to check on any possible waste of wood.

SCENARIO II — MAN WITH NATURE

The time and place are the same, but it is a different future. The place on Earth is the same, but history and the working of men's minds had been quite different. The countryside seems almost empty. On closer inspection many clusters of houses can be seen interspersed among open spaces of forests, fields, lakes, and streams. There are no overhead power lines, and roads blend into the landscape and the tall trees. Smokeless industrial parks, well landscaped, harmonize with the terrain. Parks and playgrounds are common, the air is clean, the waters are clear and blue, the houses are clean and neat, and the people are happy and serene. The land seems to be at peace with itself and with the people who live there.

Habitation gradually thins out toward the Catskill Mountain areas to the northwest and the Poconos of eastern Pennsylvania. The mountain tops and steep slopes are heavily forested with native hardwood trees. Lakes, streams, and occasional fields and villages are scattered among the mountain ridges, slopes, and valleys. Timber operations are proceeding on the lower and the gentler slopes, but they too seem to be an integrated part of the total mountain environment. An observer from the air can see little logging disturbance or scars on the terrain. The maintenance and protection of a diversified forest environment, and the protection of the land and waters, enhances the native wildlife and fish populations. People love and enjoy these mountain regions, and fishing, hunting, hiking, and nature study are common. The unobtrusive rural-type roads are numerous, with most areas being accessible by the small Peoplecars or cycles of various kinds. But people pressure on the forested areas is light. The pollution disasters of the 1980s finally convinced the country that pollution control was an imperative and vitally serious business. The three-day war in 1994 decimated the population to about half of its former size. The disasters from pollution and war made "believers" of the American people. They adopted a new life style, using technology and population control to achieve human and spiritual values rather than the former materialistic goals for an ever-increasing population.

A forester who graduated from the State College of Environmental Forestry in the class of 2043 had roamed as a boy in the forests and fields and found delight and amazement in the now almost healed natural world. The processes of nature and the biological and physical interrelationships aroused his budding scientific curiosity, so he determined to go to forestry school and major in silviculture and ecology. At the time of his graduation much of the mountain and back-country forest land was in public ownership — national forests, parks of various kinds, recreation areas, and wilderness areas.

Yet, over half of all forest land was in private ownership, mostly relatively small tracts of less than two hundred hectares. Much of this forest land was owned by professional or business people who loved the forests and liked the idea of owning land. They were highly motivated to engage in ecologically sound forest practices to enhance the different values of the forest in an integrated way. This requires professional knowledge and skills, and so there developed in the country a strong demand for consulting foresters who understand the forest as an ecosystem and who know how to protect, maintain, and manipulate it for the wildlife, timber, recreation, watershed, and aesthetic values desired by most owners. Because of these considerations, our forester started his own practice of consulting forestry.

To meet the objectives of most owners, and the social demands of the population, there had developed the kind of intensive forestry proposed by the Sierra Club and a few forward-looking foresters more than seventy-five years earlier. This included four characteristics: (1) a sustained annual or periodic yield of forest products and values, (2) maintenance of a continuous forest cover through partial cuttings to harvest mature trees and obtain regeneration, (3) trees grow to large sizes and high quality before cutting, and (4) extreme care is exercised to avoid site damage. In addition, intensive measures were taken to enhance game food and habitat and maintain a balance of unusual and ornamental trees. The woodlands were generally diversified and ecologically stable. The public and consulting foresters kept them that way.

Thinning and improvement cuttings were used as a tool to promote growth of the quality sawtimber and veneer trees and to manipulate the forest environment for non-timber uses. Wood for fiber production was taken almost entirely from these intermediate cuttings. Because of the former decreasing timber supply and pollution problems paper and paper-like materials were no longer the ubiquitous products they had been seventy-five years earlier. Thus, most of the need could be supplied from intermediate cuttings. But pulpwood stumpage prices were good, and they encouraged intensive use of thinning and improvement and salvage cuts to improve and manipulate the forest. Starting about the year 2020 there had developed a virtual revolution in tree-harvesting methods and machinery based on the need for light partial cuts, full protection of the site, and protection of the remaining trees and vegetation and the whole forest environment. This was commonly called the "sky hook" method. The trees were felled, all unwanted branches and twigs lopped close to the ground, and the useable wood lifted clean away and moved to nearby concentration yards by non-polluting flying trucks, derived from the earlier helicopters. Within a year after tree harvesting, except for the low stumps, it was almost impossible to tell where timber operation had been made. Careful research had shown this type of harvesting, even on steep slopes, caused no site damage and no pollution or trash in forest streams. On some level lands light ground machinery was still being used to move out the logs and other wood products.

On a strictly financial basis these modern methods of harvesting cost much more than the former "efficient" methods, as previously described. Yet the new life style of the people had evolved a whole new value system — a new concept of economics. Integrated use of the forests and the non-timber social and spiritual values were paramount. It was not considered a sacrifice to spend money to develop and preserve them; quite the contrary. The value system of this society demanded this course of action, and the reduced population and more sophisticated science and technology made it possible.

So as our forester worked in the forests day after day, his world was a dimension removed from the other world. The open forested spaces had come almost full circle to a period of ecological climax forests common three hundred years earlier. Yet there were important differences and significant improvements from the standpoint of humans. Diversity and stability were everywhere but trees were more vigorous than formerly, and dead and deformed trees were virtually absent. Each tree had adequate space to grow; thus crowns were full and healthy. Species composition was balanced to include special food and shelter trees for wildlife. Newly cut small openings and patches contained browse for a properly adjusted deer population. The variability of species, ages, tree sizes, and sites allowed diversity even on small areas to provide wildlife habitat for many species and a pleasing vista for nature lovers. Somehow there seemed to be a large number of flowering shrubs along paths, special recreation areas, and streams. The streams were crystal clear; the stones on the bottom had sharp, bright colors and clean surfaces; and brook trout streaked across the pools and up the riffles. The forest environment was in tune with nature while still serving man's needs. To the people it was very beautiful. These could be the forests of the future.

These larger matters will ultimately be settled by events far removed from present concerns for your woodland. But a start must be made, and tactics to save woodlands now should be briefly discussed.

FOREST ECOTACTICS

It seems clear that no significant progress in saving and improving the rural and suburban environment can occur unless the whole country participates. We cannot save open space and enhance uses of the forest community if this community is constantly under the threat of being eradicated by the works of Man or destroyed by erosion and pollution. The whole people — city, suburban, and rural — must want the open space and work together to maintain it. This, of course, must involve a quiet revolution in thinking and life styles in order to succeed. In the long run the scenarios just presented will be modified, but both kinds of worlds cannot exist in the same time and place.

Consider the present movement to the country, the continuing expansion of suburban sprawl. People move to rural-type areas because they like it there. In the absence of controls, a program to make rural areas more attractive would increase the flow of people to those areas; the more improvement the more people. Thus, rural beautification is self-defeating *unless* accompanied by controls which consider population, industrialization, pollution of all forms, roads, power lines, and all things which help determine the quality of life. If people have a beautiful lake, or a serene wooded countryside, they will "love it to death" unless constrained by some kind of government or community action. Your tactics to improve and beautify your woodland may not suffice in the long run without great cooperation from the whole human community.

Why can we not find simple and easy solutions to our problems? Why do we tend to treat symptoms and to seek piecemeal solutions? Why do we fail to recognize that the apparent solutions may create entirely new problems that were not anticipated? Why do we not recognize that partial solutions are often dangerous? Why are our priorities so often badly askew? No one can answer these questions fully, but it seems apparent that men do not fully understand the interacting forces and the dynamic behavior of their world. What is even worse, many men in authority do not even recognize the existence of such behavior. In a world with greater and greater complexity, traditional or intuitive responses to problems are not enough. Piecemeal measures to relieve pollution or other social pressures may only postpone, and make more acute, the evil day. At present we are making no significant progress overall. We have reached the end of an era — an end of easy solutions, virgin lands, an unpolluted environment, and rapid growth. The transition from this growth phase to a condition of equilibrium will be very difficult. It may not be possible without great tragedies and catastrophes. To forestall this we must develop a true "ecological conscience" and some means (probably computers) to handle the vast amount of complex data which will be involved.

In this transition period, in the context of a grim environmental future, how should you consider your own woodland? I would say consider your own lifetime enjoyment and possibly that of your children (if you can teach them to love the land). You can also consider the increased market value to you and your heirs of a well-managed and improved woodland environment. Assuming inflation and the increasing value of a quality environment, this may well be a sound financial investment. When you realize that in fifty years or less your whole woodland may be destroyed, or preempted for other intensive uses, the above attitudes are about the only ones left to you. The only sure thing is to do it for yourself, hoping that your action will later benefit others.

An example of saving open space can be cited. A group of ten families owned about 1,500 contiguous acres on the northwestern margin of a large eastern city. This was rolling farm and forest land with fields, woodlands, and streams interspersed in a rather typical pattern. Woodlands dominated the steep slopes, ridges, and stream margins, while pastures and fields occupied the flats and gentler slopes. The area had formerly been entirely farmer owned, but in the last decade several tracts had been purchased for country estates and several new houses had been built. Yet the area retained the essential character of open space, forests, and fields.

During the last two decades suburban housing had crowded right to the margin of this section of countryside. The owners of the open space were beginning to look askance at the waves of new houses along with the deforestation, pavement, and bulldozed terrain. The open space of this part of the county had long been used for hunting, fishing, hiking, bird watching, and activities of youth and outdoor groups. This had been mild pressure — people were generally considerate, and there was mutual respect and appreciation between the land owners and people of the nearby populated areas.

But all this changed rather quickly. The state formally proposed to straighten and widen the old rather winding blacktop road through the area and build new paved feeder roads to make the area more accessible. The former gravel country roads, many tree-lined, would be replaced by roads designed more for automobiles than people. In addition, the county zoning board had a petition to zone the area for single-family houses, with a half-acre minimum lot size, and spot zoning for small business. The petition was backed by powerful financial interests in the nearby city. At the same time an even more ominous development occurred in the county legislature. Open land near the city had previously been taxed on a "use" basis; the assessment had been based on the actual use of the land, mostly farming and forestry. A bill was introduced in the legislature to make assessments on the "value" of the land. Because the land was so attractive and so near the city the market value was high. Taxes based on such value would, in most cases, force the owners to sell to housing developers or land speculators. Developers were already offering tempting prices to the woodland owners for large chunks of land accessible to the present and proposed roads.

The owners of the open space were split in their initial reaction to these developments. Three of them wanted and needed the money from sale of land at high prices. But most preferred open space and a way of life to the easy money, and some were fighting mad. They deeply resented the power plays to despoil the beautiful countryside and, in effect, force them out of it. They realized that the 1,500-acre area was a unit. Either it would all be saved for open space or it would all eventually succumb to bulldozers and suburban sprawl. If it were to be saved it must be saved now and saved altogether.

At first only two or three of the owners started to fight back. They wrote letters to city and neighborhood newspapers, talked to civic groups or to whoever would listen. Fortunately, they enlisted the aid of a conservation-minded editor of a leading local newspaper. The arguments centered around the virtues of open space, how scarce it was, and how irreversible was its loss. The appeal was frankly emotional, but emotion is appropriate to many of life's situations. But it was also pointed out that, in the long run, the amenities of the open space close to the city might be far more valuable than suburbs in this particular area.

Public response to the arguments of the woodland owners was surprisingly prompt and articulate. Special interests opposed them on the grounds of growth and "progress," but a large number of people looked at the alternative and decided they would rather have open space. Encouraged by this response the ten families held a series of meetings to decide what to do. There seemed to be three alternatives: (1) keep the area in open space, fields, and forests, as at present, (2) throw it open to the usual suburban development, and (3) achieve some kind of *planned* development to maintain some open space along with housing for people. The group decided, first of all, to fight the housing development. They preferred to keep things as they were but recognized that this might be impossible. The owners decided on the following course of action: (1) continue the endeavors to enlist public support, (2) start a campaign to raise money, and (3) hire an experienced lawyer to lobby for and advise the group. Membership was extended to any and all interested citizens of the county and before the fight was over WOE (Woodland Owners for the Environment) became almost a household word.

The first legal action was an injunction against the state to stop acquiring right-of-ways for the roads. A brochure was published and distributed by the thousands. Help was extended by the local chapters of the Sierra Club, the Audubon Society, and the National Wildlife Federation. Intensive lobbying and public pressure defeated the "value" tax bill in the legislature, at least temporarily. But the fight was not over. Some of the owners still wanted money for their land, and the hammers of population pressure and economic expediency were still poised over the concept of open space. Even the city conservationists were not satisfied because they could not tell when the dam would break and houses row on row would flood the open countryside. There was no money, no promoters, and little prospect for a planned model development; and most of the woodland owners did not want to sell their property in any event.

What was to be done? This particular case was settled by a system of scenic easements purchased by the city and county governments. The owners were allowed to live on the land as usual but with certain restrictions on uses. It was still their own land. Within limits, the public also had use of the land for recreational activities. The owners received some cash, the roads and houses were kept out, and the open space was preserved for the enjoyment and benefit of the people. In the meantime, the denial of this area for suburban housing forced some hard thinking by politicians and planners to provide other housing in more suitable places for a still increasing population. Now, ten years later, everybody, or almost everybody, is happy about the whole situation.

There are a few useful tactics that may maintain or even save your own woodland. Accept all available help from all branches of government but do not *depend* on such help to manage your woodland. Such help is almost never sufficient to do the job even when fully available. Doing the whole job depends on your own initiative. You must take the action and the responsibility while at the same time working to make your community sympathetic to your goals. You will achieve only short-term goals unless society takes measures to achieve a good natural environment overall. So you manage to increase your own enjoyment and fight a rear guard action. There is always the possibility that your woodland can and will form a nucleus for open space in a more rational future society. You cannot trust government alone because government does no more than reflect public opinion, with a position often behind public opinion and always behind the best information. At present only the most advanced segments of the public understand the issues underlying the quality of life. You can use tactics to bring satisfactions to yourself and your family in the short run.

The best tactic is to create a biologically sound woodland ecosystem. Make your woodland something special. The methods and ideas for this are outlined in the previous chapters. You deserve the help and protection of society in this endeavor but probably will get relatively little of either until attitudes change drastically. You need to know whether you are showing the way to a better future or merely postponing the inevitable. Are progressive woodland owners the fingers in a leaky dyke or are they building a new dyke? Can you help people recognize the true social value of wooded open space? You not only own a forest but you will probably want to defend it and all its values.

If you make your land attractive, you should receive tax relief for open space and be paid for scenic easements. But can woodlands and open space coexist with an over-population of automobiles and all that this represents? You can fight roads and new developments made necessary and possible by the automobile, but success is far from assured. For example, automobiles in one way or another have cannibalized 60 percent of the city parklands of Atlanta, Georgia. Parks and forests are cheap places to build roads, but the damage, once done, is irreversible. Bulldozing trees to build roads is happening all over America, and it is increasing. Concerted local action by citizens' groups can and has forced highway departments to use alternative routes less damaging to forests, water, and scenic values. It can be done. Only strict zoning or land purchases by public agencies can ease the pressure of real estate developments which eat up open space. People have a right to housing, but they also have a right to a clean, healthy, and beautiful environment.

Woodlands and other open space having fragile characteristics such as thin soils and steep slopes are a special and critical problem. Misuse can do great damage to waters and nearby areas as well as the area being mismanaged. Society owes a debt to the owner who protects such sites and should be willing to offer help. Too often Man grasps opportunities provided by technology (bulldozers for cheap logging on steep slopes) rather than first considering the protection of the site and the waters. Owners of fragile natural environments should appeal to the public and to government agencies if the area is threatened or if help is needed for protecting it. The public climate is now more favorable to such appeals than formerly.

First acquire all evidence. Then determine which of several possible courses of action you wish to follow: (1) appeal to the public through the press, (2) work for political action through zoning or other means, (3) institute lawsuits for damages, (4) obtain the backing of experts (many will offer free services), and (5) search for alternatives that do not cause site damage. In a broader framework you should work for regional planning and governing bodies covering a geographic ecosystem, such as the Hudson River Valley. This will allow problems to be attacked as a whole, not bit by bit by small units of local governmental agencies. In an informed democratic society the people are always ahead of government. That is why we have elections.

How do you cope with vandals, despoilers, and trespassers who damage your woodland values? This problem is becoming more and more acute near areas of heavy population, in the very places where environmental values should be most important. Damage to your woodland must be related to all other environmental problems of the community. Keeping your woodland clean and healthy is in the public interest. This should be made perfectly clear to the public and government groups. Enlist the support of other woodland owners, sportsmen's groups, civic organizations, and conservation groups. Encourage the use of your wooded areas by nature lovers, Boy Scouts, school groups, hiking clubs, and neighbors. They will be your allies. If necessary, post your land, catch and prosecute the despoilers, but most of all sincerely and insistently state your case and some people will listen.

As a last desperate resort to fight environmental damage and pollution you can try confrontations. Confrontations make officials angry but they at least must pay attention! The results of any kind of environmental damage when publicly displayed will receive attention. Before and after photos, displays in city hall, letters to newspapers and to officials, and well-regulated demonstrations get attention. Pollution is an obscenity; say so. Damaging the environment is social immorality; say so. Overuse and abuse of natural resources of any kind is a social and economic absurdity; say so. Ecology has been termed the subversive science. To be dead serious about the environment we need to be a little revolutionary. At this time in America we have a vested interest in our own destruction; our overriding interest in current material values imperils the well-being and even the survival of the human species in the long run. To change this direction requires an about face, a quiet revolution of thinking and action. Your woodland is a good place to start.

Assistance to Woodland Owners

A PRIVATE WOODLAND OWNER has access to many kinds of assistance in managing his forest environment. These are mostly on a state and federal level, but private consultants are also available. The actual number of specific offices offering aid throughout the eastern United States is several hundred. Later I will list the addresses of state offices and you can write to these if necessary, but locally you must depend on word-of-mouth and the *Yellow Pages* of your telephone book. Then you should phone and arrange a visit for desired information.

In the Yellow Pages, look under *Government*. You will find *Government — United States* and *Government — Name State*. Under United States and *"Agriculture Department of"* you will find such titles as: "Agricultural Stabilization and Conservation," "Cooperative Extension of Name County," "Farmers Home Administration," and "Soil Conservation Service." Under *Government — Name State* you may find a "Department of Conservation" (or of forestry) and a "State University," often a land grant college. Any or all of these agencies may be able to help you as will now be explained.

There are at least six different types of assistance in managing your woodland that can be obtained from governmental agencies. These are discussed briefly below:

1. *General information:* The Extension Service of the U.S. Department of Agriculture provides information through the Land Grant Colleges and through the County Cooperative Extension

Service. This information is communicated personally or by popularized pamphlets and meetings for small groups of landowners or various organizations and civic groups. Historically the Extension Service has been strong in agriculture but relatively weak in forestry and forest environmental matters. Do not expect direct help or answers to relatively complex environmental questions. If possible, enlist the help of individual faculty members of Land Grant or State Colleges who have a special interest in your problems. State forestry departments and extension forestry departments are listed later, but you should consult the phone book for local addresses.

The U.S. Forest Service has a division of *State and Private Forestry*. The northeastern area office is located at 6816 Market Street, Upper Darby, Pennsylvania 19082, and covers twenty states in the Northeast and Lake States regions. The southeastern area is located at 50 Seventh Street, N.E., Atlanta, Georgia 30323, and covers thirteen states in the South and Southeast. These bureaus issue publications and brochures designed to help states and private forest owners. They also work directly with state personnel, forest industry, and private forest owners. But most communication and action programs are directed through the state departments of forestry or conservation, which have already been mentioned. The "Cooperative Forest Management" program is administered by the state forestry departments, and this is the home base of the Service Foresters (Farm Foresters) who work directly with landowners. This will be discussed later.

The other activities of "State and Private Forestry" are more applicable to states, industry, and large forest land owners. They are "Advisory Management," "Cooperative Forest Fire Control," "Forest Pest Control," and "Flood Prevention and River Basin Programs." Publications or information on any of these activities can be obtained by writing to the main offices in Upper Darby and Atlanta. To date relatively little emphasis has been given to the forest environmental interests of many private woodland owners. Personal contact with your local Service Forester or a consulting ecologist or forester will usually be more rewarding.

2. *Land-use plans:* The Soil Conservation Service (SCS) of the U.S. Department of Agriculture gives direct assistance to landowners by typing the soil and making land-use plans. They are not primarily interested in the forest environment but will type the soils which should be kept in forests or planted in trees, not used

for agriculture. The SCS is also interested in water resources and all aspects of soil erosion. They should be consulted before building water impoundment or erosion control devices. They will give direct technical and engineering advice and make land-use maps. Every landowner should have an SCS land-use plan for his holding. This service is free and most worthwhile. They also have a variety of practical and brief how-to-do-it publications. State offices are listed later, but use the phone book for local offices.

3. *Financial help:* The Rural Environmental Conservation Program (RECP), formerly the Agricultural Conservation Programs (ACP), administered by the Agricultural Stabilization and Conservation Office of the U.S.D.A., provides partial payments for forest conservation practices. This is handled on a county basis through the Office of Agricultural Stabilization and Conservation. Practices approved for payments vary from county to county and from year to year. You could check the practices and payments approved through your county SCS office and determine the required procedure to obtain payments. This subsidy for conservation is well worthwhile and payments are made for a wide variety of practices. Woodland owners should use their influence to increase approved forestry and conservation practices. Agriculture has received the lion's share of subsidies, but woodland owners can make a good case for help in managing forests for integrated uses and preserving open space close to populated areas. Your local or nearby office is in the Yellow Pages of your phone book.

4. *Direct technical help:* Your area Service Forester (Farm Forester) will visit your woodland, appraise it, make a plan, and mark trees for cutting if needed. This service is free. This program is directed by the U.S.D.A. Forest Service and administered by state forestry or conservation departments, usually through the State Forestry Department. This is the Cooperative Forest Management program financed jointly by the federal and state governments. Area offices usually include several counties. If the office is not in your phone book, contact the State Division of Forestry or State Conservation Department (see list) for location of your area Service Forester. This is the chief source of free professional forestry services available to you and most worthwhile if you make sure the forester understands your objectives of management. In some regions Service Foresters are heavily oriented toward timber production and do not understand or sympathize with environmental or integrated uses. Make sure the management plan and

tree marking will provide what you want.

5. *Fire protection and planting stock:* Many State Forestry and Conservation Departments have agencies for forest fire detection and suppression on private lands which are active during fire seasons. When National Forests are nearby, this work may be done in cooperation with the Forest Service. Detection of fires is by aircraft, fire towers, and by reports from citizens and fire wardens. Suppression crews are available during fire seasons. These services are free, and you should cooperate to the fullest. Planting stock for reforestation can be purchased through the State Forestry or Conservation Department (see list) of most states, at very reasonable cost. In some cases they will also give you advice about what and where to plant. As pointed out in Chapter 5, correct planting practice is essential for success.

6. *Assistance in fish and game management:* Many states have departments of fish and game, usually in the same Conservation Department as forestry. They provide fish for stocking ponds and streams, give practical advice to landowners, stock game in new areas, and help formulate the fish and game laws. Seek their advice and help wherever possible. Fish are usually free if your pond meets specifications. If you build a favorable woodland habitat for scarce game, turkeys for example, and adjoining areas are also favorable, your area would receive high priority in any restocking program. A list of state offices for fish and game assistance is given later. Check your phone book for the local office under state government.

The alternative to free government assistance is the employment of consulting foresters and resource managers. A paid consultant who is an expert in the field, and who understands your problems, will usually give you better service and produce better results than the exclusive use of free public services. The public assistance is helpful but should often be supplemented by a consultant. Consultants qualified in environmental forestry, however, are still scarce. Until recently, the demand was mostly for consulting foresters for timber and logging enterprises. As the demand increases, however, more environmental-type consulting services should become available.

It seems the woodland owner may be offered public help almost to the point of confusion. Therefore the following summary has been prepared to help simplify, or at least clarify, the complexities of public assistance to woodland owners. In most cases the related federal agencies are located in the same U.S.D.A. county office. The state agencies usually have their own offices.

Public Agency	*Services Available*
State Department of Forestry or Conservation, both state and local offices.	Direct technical help in your woodland; cooperative fire protection; tree planting stock; advice on procedures for dealing with other government agencies.
State Fish and Game Departments, often in a conservation department with forestry, both state and local offices.	Assistance in fish and game management including stocking; will give free advice and free stocking in some cases.
State University or Land Grant College, home of the Extension Forester of the U.S.D.A. Cooperative Extension Service; there may be other extension foresters located elsewhere in the state.	Publications and group meetings for farmers, landowners, and others interested in forestry; answer written and oral questions; provides mostly general material, seldom direct technical help.
U.S. Forest Service State and Private Forestry, two eastern areas.	Assistance through the states; direct assistance to landowners through publications and meetings.
U.S.D.A. Agricultural Stabilization and Conservation county offices.	Payments for approved woodland practices through the Rural Environmental Conservation Programs (RECP).
U.S.D.A. Cooperative Extension county offices; the head is sometimes called the "County Agent."	Mostly devoted to agriculture, but will give advice on how to proceed in getting help in forestry; the Extension Forester is located at a state university.

U.S.D.A. Soil Conservation Service, county and state offices.

Direct help in making land-use plans and soil surveys; direct engineering help in building ponds and all kinds of erosion control devices; direct help in water resource projects; publication of brief and practical how-to-do-it guides.

STATE FORESTRY OR CONSERVATION DEPARTMENTS

Names and addresses may change with time. These lists of addresses were adopted from the information in "Woodlands for Profit and Pleasure," by Reginald O. Forbes, American Forestry Association.

Alabama — Division of Forestry, 64 North Union Street, Montgomery 36104

Arkansas — Arkansas Forestry Commission, P.O. Box 1940, 3821 West Roosevelt Road, Little Rock 72203

Connecticut — State Park and Forest Commission, Hartford 06115

Delaware — State Forestry Department, 317 South State Street, Dover 19901

Florida — Florida Forest Service, Collins Building, Tallahassee 32304

Georgia — Georgia Forestry Commission, P.O. Box 319, Macon 31202

Illinois — Department of Conservation, State Office Building, Springfield 62706

Indiana — Division of Forestry, Department of Natural Resources, State Office Building, Indianapolis 46204

Iowa — Iowa State Conservation, State Office Building, Des Moines 50319

Kentucky — Division of Forestry, New Capitol Annex, Frankfort 40601

Louisiana — Louisiana Forestry Commission, P.O. Box 15239, Broadview Station, 5150 Florida Boulevard, Baton Rouge 70815

Maine — Maine Forest Service, State House, Augusta 04330

Massachusetts — Division of Forests & Parks, Department of Natural Resources, Government Center, 100 Cambridge Street, Boston 02202

Michigan — Department of Natural Resources, Steven T. Mason Building, Lansing 48926

Minnesota — Division of Lands and Forestry, Department of Conservation, Centennial Office Building, St. Paul 55101

Mississippi — Mississippi Forestry Commission, 1106 Woolfolk Building, Jackson 39201

Missouri — Missouri Department of Conservation, North Ten Mile Drive, Box 180, Jefferson City 65101

New Hampshire — 318 State Office Building, Capitol Street, Concord 65101

New Jersey — Bureau of Forestry, 713 Labor and Industry Building, Trenton 08625

New York — Division of Lands and Forests, New York State Environmental Conservation Department, State Office Buildings Campus, Albany 12226

North Carolina — Division of Forestry, P.O. Box 2719, Raleigh 27602

Ohio — Division of Forestry and Reclamation, Ohio Departments Building, Columbus 43215

Oklahoma — Forestry Division, State Board of Agriculture, Capitol Building, Oklahoma City 73105

Pennsylvania — Bureau of Forestry, Pennsylvania Department of Forests & Waters, Education Building, P.O. Box 1467, Harrisburg 17120

Rhode Island — Division of Conservation, Department of Natural Resources, 83 Park Street, Providence 02903

South Carolina — State Commission of Forestry, P.O. Box 287, Columbia 29202

Tennessee — Division of Forestry, Tennessee Department of Conservation, 2611 West End Avenue, Nashville 37203

Texas — Texas Forest Service, College Station 77843

Vermont — Department of Forests and Parks, Montpelier 05602

Virginia — Virginia Division of Forestry, P.O. Box 3758, Charlottesville 22903

West Virginia — Department of Natural Resources, State Office Building #3, Charleston 25305

Wisconsin — Department of Natural Resources, Division of Conservation, Hill Farms State Office Building, P.O. Box 450, Madison 53701

U.S.D.A. COOPERATIVE EXTENSION SERVICES, EXTENSION FORESTERS

These are land grant colleges, and the locations will not change.

Alabama — Auburn University, Auburn 36830

Arkansas — University of Arkansas, Fayetteville 72710

Connecticut — University of Connecticut, Storrs 06268

Delaware — University of Delaware, Newark 19711

Florida — University of Florida, Gainesville 32601

Georgia — University of Georgia, Athens 30601

Illinois — University of Illinois, Urbana 61801

Indiana — Purdue University, Lafayette 47907

Iowa — Iowa State University, Ames 50012

Kansas — Kansas State University, Manhattan 66502

Kentucky — University of Kentucky, Lexington 40506

Louisiana — Louisiana State University, University Station, Baton Rouge 70803

Maine — University of Maine, 118 Deering Hall, Orono 04473

Maryland — University of Maryland, College Park 20740

Massachusetts — University of Massachusetts, Amherst 01002

Michigan — Michigan State University, East Lansing 48823

Minnesota — University of Minnesota, St. Paul 55101

Mississippi — Mississippi State University, State College 39762

Missouri — University of Missouri, Columbia 65202

New Hampshire — University of New Hampshire, Durham 03824

New Jersey — College of Agriculture and Environmental Science, New Brunswick 08903

New York — Cornell University, 114 Fernow Hall, Ithaca 14850

North Carolina — North Carolina State University, Raleigh 27607

Ohio — Ohio State University, 1827 Neil Avenue, Columbus 43210

Pennsylvania — Pennsylvania State University, 111 Ferguson Building, University Park 16802

Rhode Island — University of Rhode Island, Kingston 02881

South Carolina — Clemson University, Clemson 29631

South Dakota — South Dakota State University, Brookings 57006

Tennessee — University of Tennessee, P.O. Box 1071, Knoxville 37901

Texas — Texas A & M University, College Station 77843

Vermont — University of Vermont, Burlington 05401

Virginia — Virginia Polytechnic Institute and State University, Blacksburg 24061

West Virginia — West Virginia University, Morgantown 26506

Wisconsin — University of Wisconsin, 111 Russell Laboratories, Madison 53706

U.S.D.A. SOIL CONSERVATION SERVICE STATE OFFICES
Names and addresses may change with time.

Alabama — Auburn University, Land Use Building, P.O. Box 311, Auburn 36830

Arkansas — 5401 Federal Office Building, Little Rock 72201

Connecticut — Mansfield Professional Building, Storrs 06268

Delaware — 501 Academy Street, P.O. Box 418, Newark 19711

Florida — 401 S. E. First Avenue, P.O. Box 1208, Gainesville 32601

Georgia — Old Post Office Building, P.O. Box 832, Athens 30601

Illinois — Federal Building, 200 West Church Street, P.O. Box 678, Champaign 61820

Indiana — 311 West Washington Street, Indianapolis 46204

Iowa — 405 Iowa Building, Des Moines 50309

Kentucky — 1409 Forbes Road, Lexington 40505

Louisiana — Suebeck Building, P.O. Box 1630, 1517 Sixth Street, Alexandria 71301

Maine — U.S.D.A. Building, University of Maine, Orono 04473

Maryland — Room 522 Hartwick Building, 4321 Hartwick Road, College Park 20740

Massachusetts — 27-29 Cottage Street, Amherst 01002

Michigan — 1405 South Harrison Road, East Lansing 48823

Minnesota — 200 Federal Building, U.S. Courthouse, 316 North Robert Street, St. Paul 55101

Mississippi — Milner Building, P.O. Box 610, Jackson 39205

Missouri — 601 W. Business Loop 70, P.O. Box 459, Columbia 65201

New Hampshire — Federal Building, Durham 08324

New Jersey — 1370 Hamilton Street, Somerset 08873

New York — Midtown Plaza, Room 400, 700 East Water Street, Syracuse 13210

North Carolina — 1330 St. Mary's Street Building, Raleigh 27605

Ohio — 311 Old Federal Building, 3rd & State Streets, Columbus 43215

Oklahoma — State Office, Stillwater 74074

Pennsylvania — Federal Building & U.S. Courthouse, Box 985, Federal Square Station, Harrisburg 17108

Rhode Island — Room 2, P.O. Building, East Greenwich 02818

South Carolina — 901 Sumter Street, Columbia 29201

Tennessee — 561 U.S. Courthouse, Nashville 37202

Texas — P.O. Box 648, Temple 76501

Vermont — 19 Church Street, Burlington 05401

Virginia — 400 North Eighth Street, P.O. Box 10026, Richmond 23240

West Virginia — 209 Prairie Avenue, P.O. Box 865, Morgantown 26505

Wisconsin — 4601 Hammersley Road, P.O. Box 4248, Madison 53711

STATE FISH AND GAME DEPARTMENTS

Names and addresses change with time. Offices are often located with forestry in conservation departments.

Alabama — Department of Conservation, 64 N. Union Street, Montgomery 36104

Arkansas — Game and Fish Commission, Game and Fish Building, Little Rock 72200

Connecticut — Connecticut State Board of Fisheries & Game, State Capital Building, Hartford 06115

Delaware — Board of Game and Fish Commissioners, Dover 19901

Florida — Game and Fresh Water Fish Commission, 620 S. Meridian Street, Tallahassee 32304

Georgia — Game and Fish Commission, Trinity-Washington Building, 270 Washington Street, Atlanta 30334

Illinois — Illinois Department of Conservation, State Office Building, 400 S. Spring Street, Springfield 62706

Indiana — Indiana Department of Natural Resources, 608 State Office Building, Indianapolis 46204

Iowa — State Conservation Commission, 300 Fourth Street, Des Moines 50308

Kentucky — Department of Fish and Wildlife Resource, Frankfort 40601

Louisiana — Wild Life and Fisheries Commission, 400 Royal Street, New Orleans 70130

Maine — Department of Inland Fisheries & Game, State House, Augusta 04330

Maryland — Department of Game and Inland Fish, P.O. Box 231, State Office Building, Annapolis 21401

Massachusetts — Division of Fisheries and Game, Department of Natural Resources, State Office Building, 100 Cambridge Street, Boston 02202

Michigan — Michigan Department of Natural Resources, Stevens T. Mason Building, Lansing 48926

Minnesota — Minnesota Department of Conservation, Centennial Office Building, St. Paul 55101

Mississippi — Game and Fish Commission, P.O. Box 451, Jackson 39205

Missouri — Missouri Department of Conservation, P.O. Box 180, Jefferson City 65101

New Hampshire — Fish and Game Department, 34 Bridge Street, Concord 03301

New Jersey — Division of Fish and Game, Department of Conservation and Economic Development, Labor & Industry Building, P.O. Box 1809, Trenton 08625

New York — Division of Fish and Game, Environmental Conservation Department, Albany 12226

North Carolina — Wildlife Resources Commission, Raleigh 27602

Ohio — Department of Natural Resources, 907 Ohio Departments Building, Columbus 43215

Oklahoma — Department of Wildlife Conservation, P.O. Box 53465, Oklahoma City 73105

Pennsylvania — Pennsylvania Fish and Game Commission, Harrisburg 17120

Rhode Island — Division of Conservation, Department of Natural Resources, Veterans Memorial Building, 83 Park Street, Providence 02903

South Carolina — Wildlife Resources Department, P.O. Box 167, Columbia 29202

Tennessee — Game and Fish Commission, P.O. Box 9400, Ellington Agricultural Center, Nashville 37220

Vermont — Fish and Game Department, Montpelier 05602

Virginia — Commission of Game and Inland Fisheries, P.O. Box 11104, Richmond 23230

West Virginia — Game and Fish Division, Department of Natural Resources, Charleston 25305

Wisconsin — Department of Natural Resources, Box 450, Madison 53701

B

Sample Timber Sale Contract

THIS AGREEMENT made and entered into this _____ day of _____, 1974, by and between:

JOHN B. DOE, an individual residing on Forest Road, R.D., Box #125, Woodsview, New York, hereinafter referred to as the Seller;

and

JOHN A. SMITH, an individual with offices and residence at 100 Prospect Street, Woodsview, New York, hereinafter referred to as the Buyer.

WITNESSETH:

1. The Seller hereby sells and the Buyer hereby buys the 267 timber trees marked with orange-colored paint spots located on the lands of the Seller situate in Lot #7, Town 3, Range 7, on and near Forest Road in the Town of Woodsview, County of Hillands, State of New York; and further described as the timber with said orange-colored paint spots or X marks on 123 cull trees in the sale area as described on the map entitled, "Doe Timber Sale" which is attached to and hereby made a part of this agreement.

2. The Seller agrees to allow the Buyer, his agents and employees to enter upon said premises for the purpose of removing or felling the marked timber therefrom and to do such other things as may be necessary in connection with the operation, including the right and privilege of the Buyer to use sufficient and necessary space in and upon said land to handle, load and haul all timber contemplated in this agreement and no other, subject to the following:

197

Log landings can be constructed and used on the sale area as indicated on the attached map. The Buyer must confine the hauling of logs to the roadway noted on the attached map and marked on the ground with red flagging.

3. The Seller reserves the right to suspend any part or all of the logging activities of the Buyer whenever, in the judgment of the Seller, such activities, due to inclement weather conditions or poor logging practices, are injurious or harmful to the property of the Seller.

4. The Buyer makes a lump sum payment, in full, of TWENTY-THREE HUNDRED SIXTY-FIVE DOLLARS ($2365.00) for all timber included in this agreement; estimated to be 59,125 board feet International Scale; and payment is to be made at the time of the execution of this agreement, the receipt of which is hereby acknowledged.

5. The Buyer further agrees to cut and remove or fell said timber in accordance with the following conditions:

(a) All timber shall be removed before the expiration of two (2) years from the date of this agreement. Any and all timber or material remaining after that time shall become the property of the Seller.

(b) Only trees under the terms of this agreement shall be cut; and the said Buyer shall pay, as liquidated damages, twenty dollars ($20.00) in cash in excess of stumpage value for each marketable tree that is cut or wantonly injured in violation of the terms of this agreement; provided, however, the Buyer shall not be liable for this penalty in felling trees when making necessary skidways or where trees have become unavoidably lodged or tops broken in felling. However, if such unmarked trees are cut the Buyer will pay the Seller the same stumpage value per unit as for the marked trees, $40 per thousand board feet.

(c) Young trees shall be protected against unnecessary injury. Only dead or the lesser valuable trees may be used for construction purposes in connection with the logging operation, and all existing roads shall be kept clear of tops and other obstructions.

(d) All hung trees will be put on the ground.

(e) Trees marked with an X are cull trees and must be felled by the Buyer, or he may remove them without cost if he considers them merchantable.

(f) No trees will be felled in or across the stream known as Cool Brook. Skidding across this stream will be done in only the one place marked on the "Doe Timber Sale" map.

(g) All roads and skid trails must be kept clear of treetops. Any treetops falling on such roads or trails must be removed before completion of this job. Treetops falling outside the boundaries of this ownership must be pulled back onto property.

(h) Along the roads and trails marked on the "Doe Timber Sale" map the felled tree tops must be lopped back to the ground. This will be done for a distance of 200 feet each side of the designated trails and roads.

(i) Skid trails should be located to have no greater than a 20 percent gradient.

(j) Upon the completion of logging operations, the Buyer shall smooth the ruts out of the skid roads, log landings and truck roads; and install water bars wherever necessary. In addition, the Buyer must repair any culvert which may have become damaged during the logging activities.

(k) The Buyer will refrain from crossing the picnic area; and will build a short road south of the picnic area, as indicated on the attached map.

6. The Buyer shall use due care to prevent fires.

7. The Buyer shall furnish the Seller with a performance bond, guaranteeing the performance of the Buyer of all conditions under this agreement; or deposit with the Seller's Agent, William H. Forest, Consulting Forester, _____, _____, New York, the sum of TWO HUNDRED DOLLARS ($200.00), cash or check, which sum may be used by the Seller to apply on damages sustained by the Seller under any violation by the Buyer of any terms and conditions of this agreement. Any sum or sums so applied shall become the property of the Seller. Upon completion of this agreement, any unused portion of said sum shall be returned to the Buyer.

8. The Buyer shall provide the Seller with a certificate for a public liability insurance policy with minimum limits of one hundred thousand ($100,000) in the event of death or injury to one (1) individual, and three hundred thousand dollars ($300,000) in the event of death or injury to more than one individual; and property damage insurance with minimum limits of twenty-five thousand dollars ($25,000) and an aggregate of fifty thousand dollars ($50,000) before this agreement is in effect.

(1) The area shall be kept reasonably clear of all trash, cans, and other litter. After logging is completed all trash and litter shall be removed.

9. This agreement shall be void and of no effect unless the

Buyer shall secure and keep in effect compensation insurance for the benefit of, and keep insured during the life of this agreement, such employees as are required, by the provisions of the Workman's Compensation Law.

10. Notice of intention of the Buyer to begin the removal of said timber shall be given to the Seller before any logging activity is begun.

11. This agreement and all provisions, terms and conditions thereof shall likewise be binding upon the parties hereto, their legal representatives, and successors.

12. This agreement is not assignable.

IN WITNESS WHEREOF, the parties hereto have set their hand and seals the day and year first above written.

By _____ (L.S.)
           John B. Doe

By _____ (L.S.)

---

*Adapted from contracts provided by, and with the assistance of, Curtis H. Bauer, Consulting Forester, 328 Wellman Building, Jamestown, New York. This sample contract gives guidelines, but the specific provisions of any contract will depend on the conditions present on a particular sale. In most cases an attorney should be consulted to check the contract in a given situation and for a particular place.

C

Helpful References

This is a list of references containing specific information on a variety of subjects of interest to conservation-minded woodland owners. The six main subject areas are ecology and conservation; woodland management; woodland silviculture; wildlife and fish management; landscape, aesthetics, and recreation; and urbanized country environment. The content of each publication is briefly described and evaluated as related to usefulness for woodland owners.

ECOLOGY AND CONSERVATION

A Conservation Saga, by Ernest Swift. Washington, D.C.: National Wildlife Federation, 264 p., illus., 1967.

Next to Aldo Leopold, Ernest Swift was probably the most articulate and inspiring voice of the postwar conservation movement in America. Swift had an intimate feeling for nature and expressed it in the poetic language of the fifty or more essays in this book. The essays will take you back to pioneer days and through the development of the conservation-environmental movement to the late sixties. Each essay is a source of insight into some facet of our struggle to keep this earth a viable home for man.

A Different Kind of Country, by Raymond F. Dasmann. New York: Macmillan, 276 p., illus., 1968.

This is a book about diversity in nature and in Man's works; it explores the meaning and benefits from diversity in our lives. Dasmann deplores the trend toward uniformity in the world, shows how it is inimical to all life, and explores in depth the ways in which we can preserve diversity. Perhaps more clearly than in any other, this book shows the necessary relation between diversity and the ecological understanding and management of our resources and our lives. It is a fascinating, profound, and well-illustrated book that you will enjoy.

A Sand County Almanac, by Aldo Leopold. New York: Oxford University Press, 226 p., illus., 1949.

This is the classic book on conservation, written by a poet in prose form. Leopold, more than any other author, articulated the great new concepts in conservation which have led to our present-day appreciation of the natural world and its relation to Man. Without exaggeration, this is a great and wise book written with compassion, understanding, and a sense of ecology, which has not been surpassed. It will open your eyes to a thousand new perceptions of nature.

America's Land and Its Uses, by Marion Clawson. Baltimore, Md.: The Johns Hopkins University Press, 166 p., illus., 1972. $8.50.

This is a general treatment of land policy written for the lay reader. Perhaps because of its broad coverage and relatively short length it is more a description of land and land uses rather than policy as such. Except for the chapter on recreation there is little emphasis on the social and environmental aspects of land use.

Concepts of Ecology, by Edward J. Kormondy. Englewood Cliffs, N.J.: Prentice-Hall, 209 p., paperback, 1969.

This well-illustrated book explains the basic concepts of ecology in scientific but easily understood terms. It is especially useful for students or laymen who wish to gain an understanding of the elementary but basic biological principles underlying the field of ecology. A working knowledge of these principles is essential for correct evaluation of more popular ecological writings so common today.

Conserving Natural Resources, Principles and Practices in a Democracy, by Shirley W. Allen and Justin W. Leonard. New York: McGraw-Hill, 3rd ed., 432 p., illus., 1966.

This is a textbook giving a survey of the general field of conservation. It is a straightforward account of resource conservation written chiefly for college freshmen. It covers the elementary aspects of this field.

Ecotactics: The Sierra Club Handbook for Environmental Activists, edited by John G. Mitchell and Constance L. Stallings. New York: Pocket Books, 288 p., paperback, 1970. $ .95.

This is a series of statements by crusading conservationists and with an introduction by Ralph Nader. It is almost revolutionary in tone and activitist in content. It highlights the many environmental problems of our times and provides rather definite suggestions on how ordinary people can attack these evils; and this book leaves no doubt that they are evils.

Environmental Conservation, by Raymond F. Dasmann. New York: John Wiley, 2nd ed., 375., illus., 1968.

This is a textbook treatment of conservation written for lower-division college levels. It is written from the biological standpoint by an ecologist who takes the long view. It touches all the conservation bases, including rather straightforward accounts of soil, water, forests, livestock, wildlife, recreation, the urban environment, and human population. It is a good source for the beginner who wishes a firm foundation in conservation.

Environmental Management Science and Politics, edited by Norton and Marsha Gordon. Boston: Allyn and Bacon, 548 p., illus., 1972.

This is a "second generation" environmental book concerned not so much with identifying the problems as with methods of environmental management to help solve them. It is a series of many essays on nearly all aspects of the environment by authorities in the fields. The writing is semi-technical, but careful reading will reward the reader with new insights into our earthly home and some of the ways we must come to terms with it and its fragile nature.

Resources and Man. The Committee on Resources and Man. National Academy of Sciences. San Francisco: Freeman, 259 p., paperback, 1969. $2.95.

A series of eight solid and rather technical reports on world resources with considerable emphasis on the relations to people. The subjects cover food from the land and the seas, minerals from all sources, energy resources, and human populations and the human ecosystem. This is more a book of factual knowledge than of insights and ideas.

The Environmental Crisis, edited by Harold W. Helfrich, Jr. New Haven, Conn.: Yale University Press, 187 p., paperback, 1970. $1.95.

This is a collection of twelve perceptive and fascinating essays by authorities in the field of ecology, especially oriented toward "man's struggle to live with himself." Each author discusses a separate subject, but each subject is vital to an understanding of our ecological predicament. Subjects ranging from weather modifications to the gross national product are explored in depth and with considerable verve. The essays by Ian McHarg, Paul Ehrlich, and Kenneth Boulding alone are worth the price of the book.

The Environmental Handbook, edited by Garrett De Bell. New York: Ballantine Books, 367 p., paperback, 1970. $ .95.

The major portion of this book is a collection of essays and excerpts by many distinguished authors explaining, often in vivid fashion, the many faces of the environmental and ecological crisis. It is useful to the amateur conservationist as a source of ideas and examples pertinent to the environmental and ecological movement philosophy. The last quarter of the book gives specific suggestions for tactics and political action to accomplish conservation objectives. This book has a wealth of environmental concepts and is one of the best of this type.

The Subversive Science: Essays Toward an Ecology of Man, edited by Paul Shepard and Daniel McKinley. Boston: Houghton Mifflin, 453 p., paperback, 1969.

This is a series of hard-hitting and imaginative essays on Man in relation to his environment. This book is notable for its literary quality, the insights into the nature of our world, the high caliber of the authors, and the many new ideas presented. The essays are not only fascinating to read but give a history of the awakening environmental movement through the fifties and sixties. The subjects are widely diverse, but all finally relate to the long-term habitation of Man on Earth.

Woodland Ecology, by Ernest Neal. Cambridge: Harvard University Press, 116 p., illus., 2nd ed., 1958.

This little book presents an elementary treatment of woodland ecology, perhaps more from a "nature study" viewpoint than scientific ecology. It describes the intimate conditions and happenings in the forest without trying to give the whole picture. Its greatest value is to sharpen your perceptions and appreciations while in the forest.

World Dynamics, by Jay W. Forrester. Cambridge: Wright-Allen Press, 142 p., 1971.

This book discusses the opportunity for bringing world society from a state of exponential growth, an impossible situation in the long run, to some reasonable state of global equilibrium. World society behaves as a multiloop nonlinear feedback system, and direct intuitive and traditional solutions cannot work. The author describes the computer "systems dynamics" approach and calls it the next frontier in human endeavor. Based on preliminary analysis it seems that to attain equilibrium all of the following must be substantially reduced about at the same time: usage of natural resources, pollution generation, capital investment, food production, and birth rate. This may be one of the most important books published during the last decade.

WOODLAND MANAGEMENT

A New Management Rationale for Small Forest Landowners, by R. L. Marler and P. F. Graves. AFRI Research Report No. 17. Syracuse: State University of New York College of Environmental Science and Forestry; Applied Forestry Research Institute, 1974, 18 pages, free.

The statistics show that in the eastern United States about three-fourths of all commercial forest land is included in small private ownerships. This publication gives considerable background material concerning these ownerships and concludes that past governmental efforts to encourage these owners toward good management have been largely ineffective because they have not fully recognized the satisfaction and speculation objectives of most owners. If public interest is served by management then some acceptable return to the producer must be found.

Christmas Trees as a Farm Crop, by John F. Hosner and Harvey S. Woods. School of Agriculture, Southern Illinois University, 34 p., illus., 1958. Free on request.

Contains practical information on Christmas tree culture for landowners in the Midwest. Species discussed are red cedar and several species of pine. Information is given on choice of planting site, selecting species, planting methods, shearing, protection, harvesting, and marketing.

Erosion Control on Logging Roads in the Appalachians, by James N. Kochenderier. Research Paper NE-158. Upper Darby, Pa.: Northeastern Forest Exp. Station, 28 p., illus., 1970.

This bulletin describes practical methods of controlling erosion on logging roads with emphasis on proper construction of roads for continued use. Information is given on planning, location, drainage, maintenance, and care after logging. Small woodland properties should usually have one permanent, well-planned road serving a system of temporary skid roads. Most erosion on logged areas come from truck roads, skid roads, and skid trails. (Safeguards against soil and stream damage should be placed in the logging contract.)

Essentials of Forestry Practice, by Charles H. Stoddard. New York: Ronald Press, 362 p., illus., 2nd ed., 1968.

As the title suggests, this book presents the basic and practical practices of forestry for those needing an overview of forestry and of forestry techniques. It is written mostly for beginning forestry students but may be useful to the woodland owner, especially if his chief objective is production of timber products.

Forest Ownership for Pleasure and Profit, by Hardy L. Shirley and Paul F. Graves. Syracuse: Syracuse University Press, 214 p., illus., 1967.

This is a book for private woodland owners oriented more toward the business, legal, and management aspects than ecological or environmental questions. It has chapters on financing the forest estate, buying forest land, managing the property, timber marketing, and increasing timber productivity. The book is general rather than specific, is fairly conservative in outlook, and is heavily oriented toward wood products forestry.

Forestry Handbook, edited by Reginald D. Forbes for the Society of American Foresters, New York: Ronald Press, 23 sections, 1955.

This is a comprehensive technical reference book covering all aspects of forestry. It is a major reference book for forestry and is packed with information on twenty-three subjects or aspects of forestry, including sections on wildlife management, watershed management, and forest recreation as well as the more commodity-oriented forestry. This is a technical reference book useful for factual information but is not easily used by laymen, has little environmental concern, and is out of date in some respects.

"Forestry, Small-Ownerships," by Leon S. Minckler. New York: McGraw-Hill Encyclopedia of Science and Technology, 3rd ed., p. 511-13, 1971.

This provides a condensed version of the small woodland ownership situation in the United States. Stress is placed on the dominance of small ownerships, the changing identity and objectives of owners, management for integrated uses, and assistance programs.

Forests and Flood in the Eastern United States, by Howard W. Lull and Kenneth G. Reinhart. Upper Darby, Pa.: Northeastern Forest Exp. Station, U.S.D.A. Forest Service Research Paper NE-226, 94 p., 1972, free.

This is an excellent summary of what is known about the effects of forests on floods and on erosion and sedimentation. It also briefly discusses other types of land use as compared to forests and the effects of different management methods. This bulletin traces the historical background of "forests and floods" and includes an informative section of "Summary and Conclusions" useful to the layman. Overall, this bulletin dispels most of the myths and folklore about forests and water which have so long prevailed. At the same time the complexity of the subject is made clear.

Guidelines for Stream Protection in Logging Operations, by Richard L. Lantz. Portland: Oregon State Game Commission, 29 p., illus., 1971.

Although this bulletin is written for conditions in the Northwest, the principles of road building and logging to minimize stream damage apply in the hilly regions of the East. The author shows the importance of undisturbed streams and how logging can affect streams. He then goes on to describe some of the relations between logging disturbance and dissolved oxygen, siltation, stream bank damage, and water temperature. Methods to minimize these effects are outlined.

Illinois Trees: Their Diseases, by J. Cedric Carter. Urbana: Illinois Natural History Survey, Circular 46, 96 p., illus., 1964.

This is a copiously illustrated and attractive bulletin describing in some detail symptoms and control of tree diseases. Although it is written for Illinois trees most of the species of trees occur throughout the East. It is oriented toward street and yard trees and is particularly helpful for suburban and rural homesteads.

Management and Inventory of Southern Hardwoods, by John A. Putnam, George M. Furnival, and J. S. McKnight. Washington, D.C.:   U.S.D.A. Agriculture Handbook No. 181, 102 p., illus., 1960, $ .55.

This is a detailed and valuable reference on bottomland (alluvial sites) hardwoods in the lower Mississippi Valley and throughout the South and Southeast. It not only describes forestry practices but gives a thorough description of all bottomland species and their characteristics. This is useful to woodland owners who wish to take a personal interest in their forest. Although the handbook is oriented exclusively toward timber production, the methods recommended produce a continuous and diversified forest suitable for integrated values.

Managing the Family Forest, by Gordon G. Mark and Robert S. Dimmick. Washington, D.C.:   U.S.D.A. Farmer's Bull. No. 2185, 61 p., illus., 1962, $ .20.

This bulletin covers the whole range of forestry practices from regeneration to marketing, including most regions of the country. It is basically a superficial coverage of the whole forestry situation for small woodland owners. It even includes such subjects as stacking lumber, safety in the forest, and sawtimber volume tables. It is concerned exclusively with timber management.

Permanent Logging Roads for Better Woodlot Management, by Richard F. Haussman. Upper Darby, Pa.:   Division of State and Private Forestry, U.S. Forest Service, 30 p., illus., 1960, free.

Logging without proper road construction can lead to severe environmental damage, especially soil erosion and stream damage. Well-constructed permanent roads minimize damage, make possible continued access to the woodland for sustained yields of both timber and non-timber values, and provide pleasing hiking and nature trails. This bulletin contains practical engineering information on forest road building. You will need experienced people to build your woods roads, but this bulletin will give you some understanding of the problems involved.

Shaping Christmas Trees for Quality, by G. R. Cunningham and
F. E. Winch, Jr. Ithaca: Cornell Extension Bull. 1080, New York
State College of Agriculture, 16 p., illus., 1968, $ .15.

This is a well-illustrated and practical guide for shaping Christmas trees of several species. In most cases shaping by artificial
pruning and shearing is necessary to produce high-quality trees
either for the market or your own use. This bulletin tells you how.

The Small Private Forest in the United States, by Charles H.
Stoddard. Washington, D.C.:   Resources for the Future, 171 p.,
illus., 1961.

This book speaks to the problem of the unproductive (for
timber) small private forest in this country. The book touches on
nearly every aspect of this overall problem, especially economics,
business, and government programs designed to help the small
owner. It is concluded that an expansion of present aid programs
will not by themselves solve the problems. Even in 1961 the book
hints that many woodland owners are interested in woodland
values other than timber.

Tree Diseases of Eastern Forests and Farm Woodlands, by George
H. Hepting and Marvin E. Fowler. Washington, D.C.:   U.S.D.A.
Forest Service, Agriculture Information Bull. No. 254, 48 p., illus.,
1962.

This bulletin briefly describes the most common diseases of
eastern forest tree species and gives methods of control where
these are known. Often direct control is not possible or practical
and control in a forest is best achieved through ecologically
balanced culture to maintain general forest health through diversity. This book is a good reference for specific tree diseases, their
causes, and possible control.

Tree Farm Business Management, by James N. Vardaman. New
York: Ronald Press, 207 p., illus., 1965.

This book was written to help the private woodland owner
make money from trees; it is entirely about timber and the financial aspects of growing, harvesting, and selling timber products. In

this context it is a practical and useful book for owners who expect to sell any substantial amount of timber. It covers management planning, accounting, taxes, loans, and selling procedures.
It is strictly a book about business management, as the title
suggests.

Woodlands, by J. D. Ovington. London: English Universities Press,
154 p., illus., 1965.

This is a good basic book for laymen who wish to gain an
elementary overview of forests, forest biology, and forest management. The information, and concepts apply to the world's forests,
and there are eighty-eight photographic plates to illustrate forest
types and conditions throughout the world. While timber use re-
ceives emphasis, other aspects, including wildlife, recreation, and
environmental effects, are considered. This is probably the best
short, basic, and semi-popular book available on woodlands of the
world.

Woodlands for Profit and Pleasure, by Reginald O. Forbes. Washington, D.C.: American Forestry Association, 169 p., plus 38-page
Appendix and 77-page key to identification of tree species,
paperback, 1971, $5.00.

Essentially this is an effort to condense the elements of technical forestry into one package for the use of woodland owners. It
includes details and reference material for a wide variety of forestry and related subjects, including mapping, timber cruising, com-
puting timber volumes, silviculture, marking, harvesting, marketing, details of plantation establishment, architectural plans for
summer homes, legal and tax matters, surveying, forestry instru-
ments, a key to tree identification, and much more. It is basically
a forestry handbook predicated on the assumption that woodland
owners can and will practice the art and profession of forestry, although at the same time the author recommends that professional
help be obtained. This is a good reference book for those who wish
to dig out the practical details of forestry practice, yet only the
very exceptional layman will be willing or able to practice intensive forestry with only this information. There is a chapter on
recreation, devoted mostly to the physical and practical aspects,
but the main thrust of the book is toward timber. This must be

regarded as a practical book of rather specific information but which must necessarily apply to the entire eastern United States. This book is excellent, but must be regarded as oriented toward traditional forestry and a how-to-do-it approach rather than environmental forestry and principles and concepts. Woodland owners need to see and understand the forest ecosystem and its problems and promises, not so much the traditional forestry techniques.

WOODLAND SILVICULTURE

Care of Forest Plantations on Farm Lands, by Fred E. Winch, Jr. Ithaca: Cornell Extension Bull. 867, New York State College of Agriculture, 15 p., illus., 1967, $ .10.

This bulletin contains brief and simple instructions for weeding, thinning, and pruning coniferous plantations. The instructions given are generally sound and practical.

Clearcut, by Nancy Wood. San Francisco: Sierra Club, 151 p., paperback, 1971, $2.75.

This book was written in response to the wave of clearcutting which has swept the country, especially in the last decade. It is frankly an anti-clearcutting crusade and highlights the abuses that have been practiced in the name of efficiency and commodity forestry. It includes a good deal of the history of the Forest Service in relation to its adoption of clearcutting for both western conifers and eastern hardwoods. It is not, of course, a balanced view but does a great service in pointing out the evils of clearcutting when used as a more or less universal method of silviculture with little regard for environmental values.

Ecological Forestry for the Central Hardwood Forest, by Peter A. Twight and Leon S. Minckler. Washington, D.C.:   National Parks and Conservation Association, 12 p., illus., 1972, $1.00.

Ecological forestry is considered to be methods of timber production which maintain and enhance other social values of the forest and protect the environment for ourselves and future generations. This concept is discussed and the results after twenty-two years of an actual forest management situation in southern Illinois.

It is shown that group selection silviculture combined with improvement cutting is a viable method of attaining the above objectives.

Ecological Forestry for the Northern Hardwood Forest, by Peter A. Twight and Leon S. Minckler. Washington, D.C.:   National Parks and Conservation Association, 13 p., illus., 1972, $1.00.

Ecological forestry is considered to be methods of timber production which maintain and enhance other social values of the forest and protect the environment for ourselves and future generations. Study of a large forest holding in Wisconsin where selection silviculture has been used since 1927 points the way for other landowners of northern hardwood forests. A sustained yield of timber has been produced, and the company has made a profit. The publication discusses this and the enhancement of aesthetic, wildlife, and recreation values by selection silviculture, good permanent roads, and careful logging.

"Hardwood Silviculture for Modern Needs," by Leon S. Minckler. *Journal of Forestry* 70(1): 10-17.

This is a technical article explaining and summarizing group selection hardwood silviculture which can be used for integrated uses, including timber. It is appropriate for either public or private forests but particularly suitable for small owners who want to maintain a continuous forest for both timber and environmental values. It gives a rationale for environmental forestry, past and present cutting methods, silviculture for integrated uses, requirements for regeneration in openings, and case histories of actual results after fifteen to twenty years.

Forest Planting Practice in the Central States, by G. A. Limstrom. Washington, D.C.: U.S.D.A. Agriculture Handbook No. 247, 69 p., illus., 1963, $ .50.

This is a comprehensive guide for tree planting, mostly applicable to the Central States region. It gives detailed and somewhat technical information for establishing forest plantations. It covers soil and site characteristics related to suitability of various tree species as well as the details of plantation establishment and early care. A highlight of the publication is the series of species selection guides. There is a recognition that trees have rather strict site requirements and that successful plantations require proper silvicultural practices.

Recommended Silviculture and Management Practices for Illinois Hardwood Forest Types, Revised 1972. Prepared by Illinois Technical Forestry Association, State Office Building, Springfield, Ill. 62706, 46 p., illus., $1.00.

This booklet gives specific technical instructions for managing woodlands in the general area of the Central States, but the principles also apply to Appalachian hardwood types. It was written as a professional and technical guide, but landowners can at least gain some insight into what is involved in forestry practice. The publication stresses a flexible approach to silviculture, depending on forest conditions and the objectives of the owner. It covers past practices, silvical characteristics of tree species, methods of improving degraded stands, choosing a system of silviculture, building the forest toward optimum levels, and methods of maintaining a well-stocked forest. It briefly discusses forestry in the future as an environmental practice. It is probably the most useful of the existing guides to eastern hardwood forestry.

Silvics of Forest Trees of the United States. Washington, D.C.: U.S.D.A. Agriculture Handbook No. 271, 762 p., illus., 1965, $4.25.

Prepared by the U.S. Forest Service, this is a comprehensive reference giving the characteristics of every important tree species in the United States, excluding Hawaii. For each species it shows the range and describes the climate and site, the life history, and the races and hybrids. It is the best and most complete technical reference on trees available.

The Practice of Silviculture, by David M. Smith. New York: Wiley, 578 p., illus., 7th ed., 1962.

Although this book is a college text it could serve as a reference for interested laymen on the more technical aspects of forest culture. It could at least show you some of the considerations and problems faced by professional foresters. However, the book is oriented toward timber production on larger properties and does not adequately cover environmental forestry and management for integrated uses on small ownerships. This book is the best source of information on standard silvicultural practices.

WILDLIFE AND FISH MANAGEMENT

American Wildlife and Plants, By Alexander C. Martin, Herbert S. Zim, and Arnold L. Nelson. New York: Dover, 500 p., illus., republication 1961.

This is a comprehensive guide to wildlife food habitats in the United States. It covers the use of trees, shrubs, woods, and herbs by wildlife. It is basically a reference book listing hundreds of species of birds and animals and giving the range and food preferences of each. It also lists all the chief kinds of plants and evaluates their use by wildlife.

Game Management, by Aldo Leopold. New York: Scribner's, 481 p., illus., 1933.

After forty years this is still a standard text of game management. Newer books give some of the newer management techniques and may be more useful in practical game management. But Leopold has captured the principles and basic understanding of the ecology of wildlife and practice of wildlife management. Leopold was the "father" of game management in this country. If widely practiced during the last forty years, his directions could have revolutionized our handling of wildlife in this country.

Invite Birds to Your Home; Conservation Plantings for the Northeast. Washington, D.C.:   Soil Conservation Service, U.S. Department of Agriculture, 16 p., illus., 1969, $ .25.

This is a color and black-and-white illustrated, attractive fold-out brochure on plants and plantings to attract birds to your yard and your woodland property. It describes plants and their characteristics, tells how to use them, and provides a sample plan for conservation treatment of suburban or rural houselots. This little brochure packs a lot of information.

Making Land Produce Useful Wildlife, by Wallace L. Anderson. Washington, D.C.: Soil Conservation Service, U.S. Department of Agriculture. Farmer's Bulletin No. 2035, U.S.D.A., 29 p., 1969, $ .20.

This is a practical and well-illustrated bulletin written more from the standpoint of a farmer than a woodland owner. It tells the typical farmer how he can improve wildlife and fish habitat on his farm. This bulletin is well worth reading for all its helpful suggestions and bits of information on wildlife and fish habitat.

Managing Farm Ponds for Trout Production, by Alfred W. Eipper. Ithaca: Cornell Extension Bull. 1036, New York State College of Agriculture, 32 p., illus., 1964, $ .25.

This bulletin discusses habitat requirements for trout versus warm water species, gives pond location and construction features, outlines trout biology, and details pond trout management. You may need professional advice to establish a trout pond, but this bulletin will give you a good deal of basic understanding.

Managing Woodlands for Wildlife. Upper Darby, Pa.: Northeastern Area, State and Private Forestry, U.S. Forest Service, 16 p., 1970, free on request.

This is a short, practical, and elementary but generally sound guide for improving the habitat for upland species of wildlife on small woodlands. It is shown why timber and wildlife management can be compatible, but in doing so the use of clearcut areas two to five acres in size is overemphasized. In most cases there should be a greater use of group selection forests. There is a useful sketch showing a management plan for an eighty-acre ownership. This is one of the better pamphlets on this subject put out by public agencies.

More Wildlife through Soil and Water Conservation, by Wallace L. Anderson and Lawrence V. Compton. Washington, D.C.: Agriculture Information Bull. No. 175, Soil Conservation Service, U.S. Department of Agriculture, 15 p., illus., rev. 1971, $ .15.

This is a highly illustrated bulletin showing and describing farm, water, and forestry practices which are favorable for wildlife and fish. It stresses wildlife habitat as part of a basic plan for soil and water conservation.

Shrubs and Vines for Northeastern Wildlife, compiled and revised by John D. Gill and William M. Healy. Upper Darby, Pa.: U.S. Forest Service General Technical Report NE-9, Northeastern Forest Experiment Station, 180 p., illus., 1974, free.

This is a comprehensive handbook on shrubs and vines useful in wildlife management. More than forty kinds of vegetation are described and evaluated by many different authors. For each group (alders, for example) the range, habitat, life history, use by wildlife, propagation, and management are given.

Some Shrubs and Vines for Wildlife Food and Cover, by Arthur W. Holweg. Albany: Information leaflet, New York State Department of Environmental Conservation, Division of Conservation Education, 6 p., illus., 1964.

This leaflet describes and illustrates in color twenty-seven species of shrubs and vines useful for wildlife. It includes methods of planting and maintainance and notes the species of wildlife which use each type of shrub or vine.

Wildlife Management for Beaver, Waterfowl, and Fish, by Reuben E. Trippensee. New York: McGraw-Hill, 572 p., illus., 1953.

This is a textbook and reference book for professional wildlife managers. Yet, it is useful to the layman who wishes information on some specific points. It should be used as a reference.

Wildlife Management Techniques, edited by Robert H. Giles, Jr. 3rd ed. Washington, D.C.: The Wildlife Society, 3960 Wisconsin Avenue, 623 p., illus., 1969, $10.

This is a collection of essays on the techniques of wildlife management. It is written for wildlife managers and scientists but would be useful to laymen interested in specific information about a particular subject.

Wildlife Management, Upland Game and General Principles, by Reuben E. Trippensee. New York: McGraw-Hill, 479 p., illus., 1948.

A reference book for those who wish to learn some of the general principles of wildlife management, especially as related to upland game.

LANDSCAPE, AESTHETICS, AND RECREATION

A Clearing in the Wilderness, by Hugh Fosburgh. Garden City, N.Y.: Doubleday, 134 p., illus., 1969.

This is a fascinating account of life in the northern wilderness — life in a cottage located at the edge of an old clearing with a view of water, forests, and mountains, and their inhabitants. There is much commentary on day-to-day living and the sights and sounds noticed by an interested and keen observer. The author vividly describes the seasons in the wilderness and the activities of hunting, fishing, hiking, and contemplating the many aspects of Nature. This book is worth reading just to get the "feel" of the primitive outdoors.

A Guide to Natural Beauty. Washington, D.C.:   Prepared by the Office of Information, U.S. Department of Agriculture. Misc. Publication No. 1056, 33 p., illus., 1967, $ .55.

This bulletin is full of color photographs and helpful hints on how to make your yard and surroundings beautiful. It does not give detailed plans but is full of inspiration, ideas, simple instructions, and a bit of promotion for various services of the U.S.D.A.

Design With Nature, by Ian L. McHarg. Garden City, N.Y.:   The Natural History Press, 198 p., illus., 1969.

This is one of the best of the recent books on rural and urban landscapes and Man's aesthetic relations to the whole of the natural world. McHarg exhibits a mixture of scientific insights and environmental design which is inspiring to even a casual reader, or one who merely studies the multitude of photographs, maps, and drawings. The author says the book is a "search for a way of looking and a way of doing." It could change your whole view of the Earth and all its complexities.

Forest Landscape Description and Inventories, by Burton R. Litton, Jr. Pacific Southwest Forestry and Range Experimental Station, Berkeley, Calif.: Research Paper PSW-49 U.S. Forest Service, Department of Agriculture, 64 p., illus., 1968.

This bulletin is a highly illustrated and somewhat technical treatment of forest landscapes. It carefully describes the elements of landscapes and landscape viewing with a great many photographic examples. Such concepts as panoramic, feature, enclosed, focal, and canopied landscapes are described and illustrated. This bulletin is especially valuable to those with more than a passing interest in the aesthetics of forest landscapes. It can sharpen appreciation of Nature's diverse moods and forms and help in understanding one's feelings when viewing forest landscapes.

Illinois Trees: Selection, Planting, and Care, by J. Cedric Carter. Urbana, Ill.: Circular 51, Illinois Natural History Survey, 123 p., illus., 1966.

This is a well-illustrated and rather detailed description of shade and ornamental trees, their characteristics, and their culture. It is particularly useful to the owners of suburban or rural property who wish to landscape their property. Most of the species discussed are also suitable for use elsewhere in the East.

Landscape Architecture, by John O. Simonds, New York: McGraw-Hill, 244 p., illus., 1961.

This is a comprehensive and detailed treatment of the principles of landscape architecture for students or for those who have an unusual interest in making the works of Man harmonize with the landscape. In a sense this is a technical book written by an artist, or perhaps it covers artistic design based on sound technology. Browsing this book will be a rewarding experience and will make you a better citizen of a hopefully better world.

Rural Recreation Enterprises for Profit. Washington, D.C.: Agriculture Information Bull. No. 277, U.S.D.A., 44 p., illus., 1963, $2.00.

This is a well-illustrated and rather detailed bulletin on the various aspects of establishing and managing several types of rural recreation enterprises. Running a recreation business is a complex and chancy undertaking unless you are well versed in the opportunities and pitfalls. This bulletin is full of background information and practical suggestions. Study it if you plan a recreation business.

The Hidden Forest, by Sigurd F. Olson, photographs by Les Blacklock. New York: Viking, 127 p., illus., 1969.

This beautifully illustrated book pinpoints the more intimate scenes, details, and inhabitants of the northeastern forest. The scores of breathtaking color plates capture the essence of visual aesthetic experience and will heighten your own appreciation of nature and your powers of observation. The text describes the seasons in terms of nature's peculiar response to the changing climatic conditions and to the hidden, small places in the forest. This is a book you will want to keep.

The Wild Gardener in the Wild Landscape, by Warren G. Kenfield. New York: Hafner, 232 p., illus., 1966.

This is a rather unusual book. It covers the art of naturalistic landscaping, as opposed to the more formal cultivated type of gardening and horticulture. Never does the author work with or on bare soil. He tells in considerable practical detail how to manipulate vegetation through eliminating plants, adding plants, and aiding plants. He explains how to perpetuate a desired but natural landscape through these means and through an understanding of vegetation development and behavior of plants and plant communities. He places considerable stress on vegetation management by the careful and skillful application of herbicides and tells how to do it. The book has a good deal of light humor and is easy to understand.

URBANIZED COUNTRY ENVIRONMENT

A Good Life for More People. Washington, D.C.: The Yearbook of Agriculture 1971, 391 p., illus., $3.50.

This 1971 Yearbook has a multitude of articles on many aspects of "space for living," "services for living," "production resources for living," and "issues for the future." It briefly discusses a large number of issues concerned with people living in our ever-changing and more complex and populated country.

Buying Country Property, by Irving Price. New York: Harper and Row, 1972, $5.95.

This book is full of practical hints and information on buying country property. It describes the actions required and the pitfalls facing the buyer, especially in strange places and situations. Unless you have had much experience, or have good technical and legal advice, it will be well worth your effort to read this book.

Conservation Goes to Town. Soil Conservation Service, U.S.D.A. A bound collection of eight reprints from the technical journal *Soil Conservation* from 1966 to 1971. Request from any office of the Soil Conservation Service.

This collection of articles is concerned with conservation problems in urban and suburban areas. It tells how the kind of soil affects construction of all kinds, how construction affects soil and water, and how vegetation can be used to stabilize critical areas. It shows how the principles of conservation and land use can be applied to urbanizing lands.

Grass Waterways in Soil Conservation, by M. Donald Atkins and James J. Coyle, Washington, D.C.: Leaflet No. 477, U.S.D.A., 8 p., illus., reprinted 1965.

You may have occasion to establish a grass waterway for run-off of water and this leaflet tells just how to do it, including methods and grasses to use.

Know Your Soil. Washington, D.C.:   Agriculture Information Bull. No. 267, Soil Conservation Service, U.S.D.A., 16 p., illus., revised 1970, $2.00.

This well-illustrated bulletin includes the basic facts you should know about soils before you build, excavate, or otherwise manipulate the soil for any construction or road building purposes. It will help avoid the many costly and serious mistakes commonly made.

Open Land for Urban America, by Joseph J. Shomon. Baltimore, Md.:   The Johns Hopkins University Press, an Audubon book, 171 p., illus., 1971.

The book discusses the acquisition, safekeeping, and use of open land in and near urban areas. It is based on the premise that urban environments can be made more beautiful and thus more appealing to the people who live there. Urban open space and green space and their planning, management, and safeguarding are discussed. A number of illuminating case histories involving the city, suburbs, and regional open land projects are described, including scenic easements and examples of agencies offering assistance. This is a rather elementary and down-to-earth treatment of the subject, easy to read and understand by the lay public.

Outdoors U. S. A. Washington, D.C.:   Yearbook of Agriculture, U.S.D.A., 1967. 408 p., illus., $2.75 (or perhaps free from your Congressman).

This is a volume of scores of separate articles on all aspects of outdoor recreation and natural beauty from backyards to wilderness. Hardly a subject is missing, and there are informative articles on almost anything concerned with outdoor activity and environment. This volume is indeed a treasure house of interest, ideas, know-how, and beautiful photos for any person who loves and enjoys the outdoors. Keep it on your bookshelf for constant reference.

Soil Conservation at Home. Washington, D.C.: Agriculture Information Bull. 244, Soil Conservation Service, U.S.D.A., 29 p., illus., revised 1969, $ .20.

This bulletin illustrates and discusses soil and water problems of suburban areas and how to cope with them. It is packed with tips and practical suggestions for prospective home builders and people who live in either rural or suburban areas.

Soils and Septic Tanks, by William H. Bender. Washington, D.C.: Agriculture Information Bull. 349, Soil Conservation Service, U.S.D.A., 12 p., illus., 1971, $ .15.

This is a well-illustrated bulletin which gives practical information on building septic tank systems, especially as related to the nature of the soil. Reading this bulletin will give you a good understanding of how a septic systems should be installed and how it operates.

Trees and Forests in an Urbanized Environment. A symposium. Amherst, Mass.: Cooperative Extension Service, 168 p., illus., 1971, $3.00.

This is a series of essays which discuss many aspects of the relations between trees and forests and the urbanized environment. It contains useful reference material on the social values of trees and forests, especially as related to the environmental aspects. Management of trees and wooded areas for different purposes is discussed in a general way and some attention is given to planning. This is a pioneering effort in bringing together existing knowledge on urban forestry.

Property Power: How to Keep the Bulldozer, the Power Line, and the Highwaymen Away from Your Door, by Mary Ann Guitar. Garden City, N.Y.: Doubleday, 322 p., 1972.

The old American dream of owning property is now becoming more and more difficult and complex. Those who think of land as a place to live on and love are coming into conflict with those who treat land as only a commodity. This book explores the means available to property owners to protect their property from various encroachments. The Appendices give examples of some of the common legal means which can be employed.

Landscape for Living. Washington, D.C.: The Yearbook of Agriculture 1972, 376 p., illus., $3.50.

The 1972 Yearbook is heavily illustrated and has more than sixty articles on many aspects of the use of plants for landscaping and for amenities. The subjects include plants as related to the environment, selecting and protecting plants, breeding and culture of plants, understanding plant growth, and uses of plants for landscaping in both private and public situations.

Index

Aesthetics:
    related to the forest
    environment, 106, 108-109
Appalachian mixed hardwood forest:
    description, 16-17

Beaver: habitat for, 90
Bobcat: habitat for, 90
Bottomland hardwood forest:
    description, 16, 18
Browsing deer: illustrated, 85
Bulldozer damage: illustrated, 150
Burned forest: illustrated, 145

Clearcut forest:
    illustrated, 73, 132-33;
    twelve years after: illustrated, 74
Clearcutting: 28;
    related to woodland values, 6;
    as related to sustained yield, 32;
    on steep slopes, 34;
    concept and use, 70
Climate: 16; concept of, 12
Climax types: concept of, 14
Conservation: concept of, 3-4
Continuous forest inventory:
    use of, 76
Crown ratio: concept for trees, 25
Cull trees killed: illustrated, 67

Damaged watershed:
    example of, 115-16
Damaged woodland:
    a case history, 148, 151, 154
Damaging agents:
    to the woodland, 139-40;
    control of, 140, 142, 144, 146-47
Den tree: illustrated, 89
Density:
    concept of, 25;
    how controlled, 27-28
Diversity:
    nature and occurrence, 16-17;
    value for wildlife habitat, 81-82

Earth: concept of, 1
Eastern forests:
    general nature and range, 14-15
Ecological factors: classes of, 12
Ecological stages: later, 16
Ecological succession:
    concept of, 13-14;
    reversing trend, 33-34
Ecology:
    concept of, 4, 11-12;
    general application, 34
Economic maturity:
    concept for trees, 61

Economics:
    concept for woodland owners, 36-37
Ecosystem: concept of, 4
Ecotactics:
    use for saving woodlands, 175-82;
    case history, 177-79;
    measures to use, 180-82
Eiseley, Loren: quoted, 3
Even-aged forests: concept of, 28

Fields:
    maintaining in open wild state, 104-106
Fish:
    for stocking ponds, 93;
    habitat for, 83;
    legal status of, 80
Fish and game departments:
    addresses, 193-95
Fish ponds: management of, 92-94
Fixed costs: concept of, 38-39, 42
Forest:
    concept of, 4;
    unmanaged, illustrated, 26
Forest character: control of, 27-29
Forest conservation: concept of, 4
Forest culture:
    for wildlife habitat, 82
Forest environment: concept of, 45
Forest land purchase:
    financial and legal considerations, 161-62;
    criteria for decisions, 156-60
Forest openings:
    as in group selection, illustrated, 121;
    general relation to young growth, 25;
    use in silvicultural practice, 29
Forest protection:
    steps to accomplish, 147-48
Forest soils: 13
Forest types: map of, 15
Forestry or Conservation departments: addresses, 188-90
Forests:
    of the eastern United States, 4-5

Fox: habitat for, 90
Future forests:
    speculation about, 165
Future forests scenarios:
    man vs. nature, 170-72;
    man with nature, 172-75

Game:
    concept of, 80;
    management, special measures for, 82-83
Geographic scope: 9
Girdling: illustrated, 64
Green tree reservoir: illustrated, 91
Group selection:
    concept and use, 69
Group selection forest:
    illustrated, 130-31;
    profile of, illustrated, 135
Growing stock:
    reasons to maintain, 61
Gully:
    from careless logging, illustrated, 149

Habitat:
    requirements for game species, 83-84, 86, 88-90, 92
Harmony:
    uses for wildlife, recreation, aesthetics, 124-25, 128
Herbicides: use of, 105
Human behavior:
    as influenced by forests, 45-46
Human satisfactions:
    related to economics, 36-37
Huxley, Aldous: paraphrased, 3

Immature trees: reasons to leave, 61
Improvement cutting: illustrated, 66
Integrated use:
    related to woodland values, 6-7;
    concept of, 33-34, 119-20;

economics of, 42-43;
factors and requirements for, 120, 122-24;
in a sample woodland, steps to accomplish, 135-37;
woodland, illustrated, 126-27
Interception: of precipitation, 111
Intermediate cutting: concept of, 51
Interrelations:
within the woodland, 13

Kaskaskia Experimental Forest: 39

Land: desire to own, 155
Land use:
pressure by sportsmen, 80-81
Land use plans: 184-85
Landslides: reasons for, 114

Mountain lake: illustrated, 107
Multiple use: concept of, 33

Natural regeneration:
discussion of, 61, 68
Natural succession:
concept of, 13-14
Nesting grouse: illustrated, 87
Northern coniferous forest:
description, 17, 19
Northern hardwood forest:
description, 16, 18

Oak-hickory forest:
description, 16-18
Oak-pine forest: description, 16, 18
Open-space landscape: 5
Ornamental shrubs: use of, 108
Ownership:
aspects of, 156;
objectives of, 156;
property, costs of, 161-62

Physical environment:
of the forest, 12
Pine plantation:
for site protection and timber, illustrated, 143
Pioneer species: concept of, 13-14
Pioneer types: 14
Pocket gophers:
choosing a home, 109
Pollution: in fish ponds, 93
Pond weeds: control of, 93
Property taxes: discussion of, 162
Pruning: illustrated, 65

Raccoons: habitat for, 90
Raindrops:
on forest litter, illustrated, 113
Range: concept for tree species, 21
Recreation:
related to forest environment, 99-100, 102-103;
commercial development, 100;
types of, 100;
cultural measures to maintain, 100, 102-103
Recreation areas:
damage to, 102-103
Recreation home: illustrated, 101
Recycle: need for, 3
References:
ecology and conservation, 201-205;
woodland management, 206-12;
woodland silviculture, 212-14;
wildlife and fish management, 215-18;
landscape, aesthetics, and recreation, 218-20;
urbanized country environment, 221-24
Regeneration cutting:
concept of, 51;
methods of, 68-71
Regulation: of woodlands, 75-76
Release cutting: illustrated, 63
Ruffed grouse: habitat for, 86

Rural life:
    recollections from childhood,
    166-70

Saplings:
    inforest openings, 20;
    of oak and hickory, illustrated,
    23;
    of yellow-poplar, illustrated, 22
Seed tree: concept and use, 70
Selection cutting:
    concept and use, 69
Shelterwood: concept and use, 70
Sierra Club: 173
Silvics: concept of, 21
Silviculture:
    concept of, 5-6, 11;
    practice of, 25
Single tree selection:
    concept and use, 69
Site:
    quality, concept of, 21;
    related to forest type, 16
Social values:
    generally as related to forest en-
    vironments, 45-46;
    direct benefits from forests, 47-48
Soil complex: concept of, 12
Soil Conservation Service: 92
Songbirds: habitat for, 90, 92
Southeastern coniferous forest:
    description, 17, 19
Space:
    soil and air for young growth, 25
Squirrels: habitat for, 88
Stream bank protection:
    illustrated, 141
Subsidies:
    for forest managem 'nt, 183, 187
Suburban forests: as related to social
    values, 47-48
Sustained yield: concept of, 32

Technical help:
    for forest management, 184-86

Thinning:
    concept of, 27-28
    illustrated, 62
Timber:
    yield and growth of, 43;
    costs and returns, 43;
    as social value, 50;
    yield and measurement units, 72,
    75;
    integration with other values,
    128-29, 134;
    example of integration with
    other values, 129
Timber sale contract:
    sample of, 197-200
Timber values:
    as a by-product, 37-39, 41-42;
    conflicts with other values, 129,
    134
Tolerance: concept of, 21, 24
Topography: as key to diversity, 47
Transpiration: of forests, 111
Tree classes:
    concept and definition of, 52;
    illustrated, 53-58;
    application of concept, 59
Tree planting:
    requirements for success of,
    76-77
Tree species:
    characteristics of, 12, 30-31
Tree species composition:
    how controlled, 27;
    related to natural regeneration,
    68
Tree sprouts:
    how to eliminate, 104-105
Trees in forest:
    mature and high risk, illustrated,
    60
Trout stream: illustrated, 95

Uneven-aged forests: concept of, 28
U.S.D.A. Extension Services:
    addresses, 190-91
U.S.D.A. Soil Conservation Offices:
    addresses, 192-93

U.S. Forest Service: 7, 39

Water quality:
    factors affecting, 117-18;
    objectives of, 117-18
Water values:
    integration with other values, 134
Water yield:
    factors affecting, 116-17
Watershed:
    protection of, 111-12, 114-16;
    agents that damage, 115-16
White tail deer: habitat for, 83-84
Wild turkey: habitat for, 88
Wildlife:
    composite, illustrated, 97;
    concept and general discussion,
    79-80;
    legal status, 80;
    the future of, 94, 96
Wildlife habitat:
    limitations on, 81;
    management of, 81-83

Woodcock: habitat for, 90
Woodland:
    example of yield and costs, 39,
    41-42;
    before treatment, illustrated, 40;
    before logging, illustrated, 152;
    after logging, illustrated, 153
Woodland countryside: illustrated, 8
Woodland growth rates:
    expected, 78
Woodland management:
    values from, 6-7;
    policy for, 163
Woodland
    management assistance: 183-188
Woodland owners: objectives of, 5-6
Woodland ownerships:
    importance of, 7
Woodland silvics:
    discussion of, 24-25
Woodland values:
    material and aesthetics, concept
    of, 36-39
Wordsworth, William:
    quotations, 45-46, 109

WOODLAND ECOLOGY

Environmental Forestry for the Small Owner

was composed in ten-point IBM Selectric Century
Medium and leaded two points by Metricomp Studios.
It was printed offset on fifty-five pound Perkins
& Squier's Litho paper, Smyth-sewn, and bound in
Columbia's Sierra Parima over boards by Vail-Ballou
Press, and published by

SYRACUSE UNIVERSITY PRESS
Syracuse, New York 13210